P9-ARN-649

THE COMPLETE BOOK OF
NORTH AMERICAN OWLS

THE Decatur PUBLIC LIBRARY

Purchased with the
Hosac Peter Conliss
Endowment

THE COMPLETE BOOK OF
NORTH AMERICAN OWLS

DR. JAMES R. DUNCAN

THUNDER BAY
P·R·E·S·S

San Diego, California

Thunder Bay Press
An imprint of the Baker & Taylor Publishing Group
10350 Barnes Canyon Road, San Diego, CA 92121
www.thunderbaybooks.com

Copyright © 2013 Salamander Books

Produced by Salamander Books,
an imprint of Anova Books Company Ltd.,
10 Southcombe Street, London W14 0RA, U.K.

Copyright under International, Pan American, and Universal Copyright Conventions.
All rights reserved. No part of this book may be reproduced or transmitted in any
form or by any means, electronic or mechanical, including photocopying, recording,
or by any information storage-and-retrieval system, without written permission from
the copyright holder. Brief passages (not to exceed 1,000 words) may be quoted
for reviews.

"Thunder Bay" is a registered trademark of Baker & Taylor. All rights reserved.

All notations of errors or omissions should be addressed to Thunder Bay Press,
Editorial Department, at the above address. All other correspondence (author
inquiries, permissions) concerning the content of this book should be addressed
to Salamander Books, 10 Southcombe Street, London W14 0RA, U.K.

Library of Congress Cataloging-in-Publication Data available upon request.

ISBN-13: 978-1-60710-726-2
ISBN-10: 1-60710-726-0

Printed in China.

1 2 3 4 5 17 16 15 14 13

DECATUR PUBLIC LIBRARY

OCT 0 1 2013

DECATUR, ILLINOIS

WITHDRAWN

Page 2: Great Gray Owl, the Rocky Mountains (Getty Images).

Contents

Introduction

Opposite: The Great Gray Owl is the only species of its genus to be found in both North America and Eurasia. There are estimated to be more than 60,000 worldwide.

Below: The Common Barn Owl is distinguished by its buoyant flight and long wingspan of 35–43 inches.

Owls are fascinating to us because they are simultaneously foreign and familiar. We relate to their humanlike faces, often projecting ourselves into their bodies and imagining that they think and feel as we do. Yet when we experience or try to imagine their nocturnal lives, we reach an impasse and are forced to admit much of their lives are indeed strange and beyond our reach. When owls and humans meet, it is sometimes hard to know which is more fascinated, startled, or even frightened.

I hope this book will give you greater insight into the wonderful world of these amazing birds to help close this paradoxical gap between owls and humans. Much is at stake if we do not, for the fate of owls is very much in our hands. Our planet's natural resources are currently straining to sustain over seven billion people, one of an estimated 10 to 30 million species of life on earth. Through a better understanding of other species, such as owls comes appreciation, and through appreciation comes conservation. Owls are intriguing birds, and this book will help you to better appreciate and ultimately help conserve them.

What Is an Owl?

Owls consist of a group of about 250 bird species belonging to the taxonomic order Strigiformes. Their ancient record is rich and extends back 70 to 80 million years ago. Some fossil owl species were giants compared to those alive today. One extinct ground-dwelling species, the Giant Cursorial Owl, *Ornimegalonyx oteroi,* had the most powerful talons of any owl and was 3.6 feet tall and weighed almost 20 pounds. It likely ran after and preyed upon giant rodents and perhaps ground sloths. The Elf Owl is the lightest and smallest owl, whereas the Eurasian Eagle Owl is the heaviest alive today. The closest living relatives to owls are the goatsuckers and nightjars, a group on nocturnal insect-eating birds. Owls share some features such as fleshy tongues, strongly hooked bills, strong feet, and sharp curved talons, with diurnal birds of prey (hawks, falcons, and eagles), but these evolved independently in these two groups. Owls

Opposite: Barn owls, like the one at the left, and Bay owls are distinguishable from all other owls by their heart-shaped facial disk.

Below: All Typical Owls have a rounded facial disk. This is a Long-eared Owl.

Right: The Elf Owl is the world's smallest owl. Its length ranges from 4.7 to 5.5 inches, and it weighs between 1.3 and 1.9 ounces.

and other raptors often exhibit reversed sexual size dimorphism, which means that females are usually larger than males. The Strigiformes have no crop—the expanded section of the esophagus above the stomach for storing food, common to many species of birds. They also possess two elongated, large, appendix-like pockets off their intestines called caeca.

Owls are classified into two main groups, or taxonomic families: Barn and Bay Owls (Tytonidae), which have a heart-shaped facial disk, and the Typical Owls (Strigidae) that have a rounded facial disk. Owls have an upright posture, big heads, large forward-looking eyes, and a small bill situated on a broad, flat face. Other traits atypical from most birds include the use of their upper eyelid to close their eyes or to blink. They have relatively soft feathers, large wings, and short tails compared to most other birds. A "parliament" of owls is used to describe a gathering of owls, but in reality most species tend to live alone except when breeding. They have many special adaptations that enable them to be active at night (nocturnal) and to catch prey.

The scientific classification of owl species is still in a state of flux, resulting in species lists that range from 150 to 250 species. Many of the species covered in this book were formerly thought to be subspecies of more widely distributed species. New and ongoing research that carefully examines species diversity and differences in the plumage, song, and molecular DNA of known owl populations is revealing greater species diversity than previously thought, especially in tropical ecosystems. In this manner, two new owl species were discovered, then announced, in 2012 in the Philippines, and five more Philippine owl subspecies were given full species status. The ongoing discovery of new life-forms on our planet contributes to understanding the diversity of life and our universe, and represents the cumulative effort of millions of people. This book summarizes but a slice of the human endeavor to learn about our world. I hope you use it as a springboard to making new discoveries of your own.

Below: Unlike most other birds, owls make use of their upper eyelids to close their eyes or blink. This is a Eurasian Eagle Owl.

Special Adaptations of Owls

Camouflage

Part of the owl's mystique is that they are more often heard than seen. A combination of behavior and drab feather coloration usually enables them to stay hidden from predators and prey alike. Most are a mottled mixture of various shades of brown, gray, white, and rufous colors. These colors occur in complex pattern combinations of spots, streaks, and crossbars, many of which serve to break up the outline of the owl. Furthermore, many owls possess earlike feathers atop their head, which they can lay flat or erect. While the exact function of these ear tufts is still debated among owl biologists, many believe that when erect they serve to camouflage a tree-roosting owl by making it appear like a broken-off branch or piece of bark. Where owls choose to roost by day also assists their panache for avoiding detection. Many find tree cavities to hide in, while others perch among dense vegetation or against tree trunks or among rocks and boulders. Natural selection has created some dramatic species variation across their range, reflecting the variable conditions and habitats in which they live. For example, Great Horned Owls from the dry subarctic boreal forests near the tundra are strikingly white, whereas those living in moist coastal forests are among the darkest.

One stark contrast to all this effort to hide their presence is the bright

Above and right: The Eastern Screech Owl (above) and the Great Gray Owl (right) blend into their surroundings.

Above: The bright yellow eyes of many owl species, like the Snowy Owl (above), are at odds with the camouflaging effect of their feathers. However, owls will close their eyes to make themselves almost invisible to predators.

yellow eyes possessed by many owl species. Sleeping owls hide these intense and startling yellow beacons by simply closing their eyelids. When an owl detects danger approaching, many species elongate their bodies, compress their plumage, tuck one wing wrist under their chin, and squint at the threat through almost closed eyelids. This posture changes quickly should the predator approach too closely, and the owl either flies away or erects its plumage to appear many times bigger than its actual body and contracts its pupils, maximizing the size of its striking large yellow eyes. Some species even weave, bob, and hiss to further intimidate the potential predator.

In contrast, one feather color pattern adaptation uncharacteristically draws attention to the owls that sport it. The plumage on the back of many pygmy owl species' heads looks like a face, complete with false black eyes and a black nose or beak. Predators approaching these owls from behind may be reluctant to attack if they are fooled into thinking that the owl is looking at them. In this manner the owl has a reduced chance of being ambushed while hunting by day or roosting. One study even documented that mobbing birds actually avoided the false eye spots more than the owl's real eyes, perhaps even facilitating their capture by the owl.

Hearing

There are many adaptations that help owls hear prey hidden by snow, grass, or other objects or that are simply less visible at night. The most obvious external feature is their facial disk, a special configuration of adjustable feathers that focus or channel even weak sounds into their large and asymmetrical half-moon-shaped ear openings. Depending on the species of owl, the ear openings are bordered by either rear and/or forward earflaps controlled by muscles and ligaments that can change the shape of the disk. The feathers of the facial disk form layers and vary from thin, skeletal-like feathers that keep dirt out but allow sound to pass through to those that are stiff, flat, and dense and make up the outer ruff. The ruff forms a curved or parabolic reflector-like area behind each ear. Your cupped hands placed behind your ears will make sounds louder and

Below: Owls have rear or forward earflaps (sometimes both) that are controlled by muscles and ligaments. The picture below shows the ear structure of a Long-eared Owl.

will give you an idea of how the facial disk works. The edge of the ruff is often visibly distinct along the outer edge of an owl's facial disk. The skeletal and internal structures of the owl's ear are equally specialized.

The inner ear of an owl is also relatively large, and the part of the brain that detects and processes sound is packed with more auditory nerve cells compared to other similar-size birds. Owls can hear about the same range of sound frequencies as people, but are much better at hearing sounds from about 0.5 kHz to 9 kHz. Within these frequencies it is estimated that owls can hear about ten times better than most humans.

People have symmetrical ears, meaning that they are in the same position on either side of our head. Our brain is able to process subtle differences in the volume and timing of sounds that reach our ears, a process called binary fusion. In this manner, we can perceive if an unseen sound is to our right or left. To face the sound source, we turn our heads until the sound energy and arrival time in our ears is equal. The ears on the relatively large head of an owl are far apart and asymmetrical, improving their binary fusion capacity. Owls use their internal and/or external ear asymmetry to enhance their ability to locate more precisely the location of noisy prey that they cannot see. They can perceive where the sound is both vertically and horizontally at the same time, so they can launch an attack and pounce on a grassy patch exactly where the prey was within seconds of when it made its last fateful sound.

Silent Flight

The ability to fly quietly is important for owls, to both avoid alerting prey to their attack and to ensure that the approaching owl can hear and relocate moving prey hidden by vegetation or snow. Likewise, the United States government is interested in creating an ultra-quiet Unmanned Aerial Vehicle (UAV) or drone to mimic this predatory advantage. This would allow the UAV to do its mission without being shot down by an adversary. The U.S. Office of the Director of National Intelligence invested $4.8 million in the "Great Horned Owl Program" to achieve intelligence advantage over its enemies. Such an "owl drone" could spy on enemies undetected. NASA has also examined owls' stealthy plumage for ideas for new airplane designs to reduce commercial aircraft noise levels at airports. By copying owl structures and adaptations, it may take only years for humans to re-create what evolution and natural selection has taken millions of years to perfect.

Most of us have heard birds flying overhead because of noisy, turbulent,

Opposite: Long-eared Owl. Owls use their hearing to locate what they cannot see. They perceive sound vertically and horizontally, and can launch an attack within seconds of hearing their prey.

17

Above and opposite: Owls can fly almost silently, enabling them to listen for prey while not being detected. Sound is reduced particularly by the structures of the large flight feathers on their wings. These comblike and tattered-edged feathers prevent noisy turbulence as air moves over the wings. Although owls are not the fastest birds, some, including the Barn Owl (opposite), can reach a top speed of 50 mph. Above, a Great Gray Owl prepares to land.

swirling, airflow over their wings, whereas owls fly quietly. Some people have argued that owls make less noise simply because they fly slower than other birds. However, experiments have documented that special owl feather structures create smoother airflow over the wing, and that they are quiet not just because they are slower. When owls fly, air turbulence is reduced due to a comblike serrated edge on the leading side of the outermost flight feathers. The owl's outer wing also stabilizes their flight at low speeds. However, the greatest sound reduction comes from the ends (inner vanes) of an owl's major wing—or flight—feathers, which create a tattered trailing edge to the wing somewhat like the fringed end of a scarf. This tattered edge breaks up the sound waves produced by the downstream air wakes formed as air moves over the wings.

Another source of noise made by birds results from hard wing feather surfaces rubbing against each other as the wing extends and retracts during flapping flight. However, the upper surface of owl wing feathers are velvety soft or fuzzy, thus dampening or absorbing sound frequencies above 2 kHz. This results from a reduction of friction when these feathers rub against the hard undersurface of adjacent wing feathers. You can

experience this difference by comparing the sound of your palms rubbed together, which is louder than when you rub your palms against a soft shirt or sweater.

The aforementioned feather adaptations make owls the quietest flying birds. One detailed outdoor study recorded owls and other birds flying over an array of ninety-two microphones synchronized with two video cameras. Flying owls generated less noise at frequencies above 1.6 kHz compared to other birds. Even more remarkable was that the noise from the owls at higher frequencies (above 6.3 kHz) was too quiet to measure even with the microphone array. Mice can hear sounds from 1 to 100 kHz, but are less sensitive to low-frequency sounds and very sensitive to sounds around 16 kHz. Thus, the structural adaptations of owl feathers allow these birds to fly and catch mice undetected.

Right: The velvety soft upper surface of owl wing feathers reduces noise-generating friction when they rub together during flight. The beautiful pattern at the right belongs to a Tawny Owl.

Vision

It is an old myth that owls can see in complete darkness and that they are blinded by the light of day. They do have fascinating visual adaptations that make them efficient predators who can see prey by the dim light of the stars and moon at night. Their eyes face forward and have overlapping fields of view, resulting in binocular vision. This allows them to instantly perceive the relative distance of perches, obstacles, and prey. They also have enormous eyes. The Eastern Screech Owl's eye is 4 percent of its body mass, compared to 0.08 percent for a human eye. Large eyes are important for seeing at night because they allow more light energy to fall on the light-detecting cells in the retina, the nerve-packed lining at the back of the eye. But large globular eyes are heavy, fluid-filled objects, and heavy heads are a liability to flying animals that have evolved bodies with a low center of mass. Owls have evolved tubular-shaped eyes with a light internal bony cone called a scleral ring, thus reducing the weight of their skulls while maximizing size of the image projected on the retina.

Above: Although they cannot see in complete darkness, owls can hunt efficiently by the dim light of the moon or stars. The eye above belongs to a Western Screech Owl.

Above: The Great Horned Owl has conspicuously large eyes.

The retina is the lining on the back of the eye that contains two kinds of light-detecting nerves; cones that detect color, and extremely light-sensitive rods that detect varying shades of gray. Owls have relatively more rods packed into their retinas than diurnal birds, enabling them to see better at night. There are other features of the owl eye that help them see at night, including a large maximum pupil size, large thickened cornea, and additional structures in the retina called the pectin and the fovea.

The eyes of an owl are so large that they are immobile, or fixed in the eye socket. This, combined with their narrow field of view, means that an owl must turn its head widely to look about. The underside of an owl's skull has a single round projection that acts as a swivel, where it attaches to a long neck with fourteen vertebrae. These features allow an owl to swivel its head as much as 180 degrees in each direction from a forward-looking position.

Olfaction

The area of a bird's brain used to process the sense of smell is called the olfactory bulbs. These bulbs are very small in owl brains compared to those in other birds, especially those that depend on their sense of smell for finding food, like the nocturnal Kiwi of New Zealand. Their small olfactory bulbs imply that owls do not have a well-developed sense of smell. This is perhaps supported by the fact that owls routinely kill and eat animals, such as large beetles and skunks, that excrete distasteful and odiferous chemicals that deter most other predators.

Below: Owl nostrils are located toward the base of their bills. The fact that large owls are able to hunt and eat skunks is a clear indication of their underdeveloped sense of smell. Below is a Barred Owl.

Toes and Talons

Owls use their strong feet and eight sharp claws called talons to grasp and kill a great variety of prey, including worms, crabs, insects, and other invertebrates (animals with no backbone) as well as fish, amphibians, reptiles, birds, and mammals. Owl feet and toes can exert considerable pressure, and larger prey are killed in part by constriction. The talons also play a role in killing prey by puncturing vital organs. The middle talon has a cutting edge, or groove, that perhaps accelerates the death of prey by letting blood flow out of the wound. This is sometimes called the scraping claw, as owls also use it to clean their bills after eating. The pressure exerted by the feet and talons of the Great Horned Owl ranges from 300 to 3,000 pounds per square inch (psi). This is considerably greater than the 20 psi exerted by an average person's grip. Despite the killing power of an owl's formidable feet and talons, smaller prey are often quickly given a "coup de grâce" bite to the head to quickly dispatch them. After all, even small rodents can bite back and inflict wounds that may become infected.

Most birds have three toes pointing forward and one hind toe (called the hallux) pointing backward. Owls have the ability to rotate the outer toe

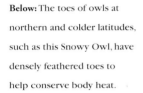

Below: The toes of owls at northern and colder latitudes, such as this Snowy Owl, have densely feathered toes to help conserve body heat.

24

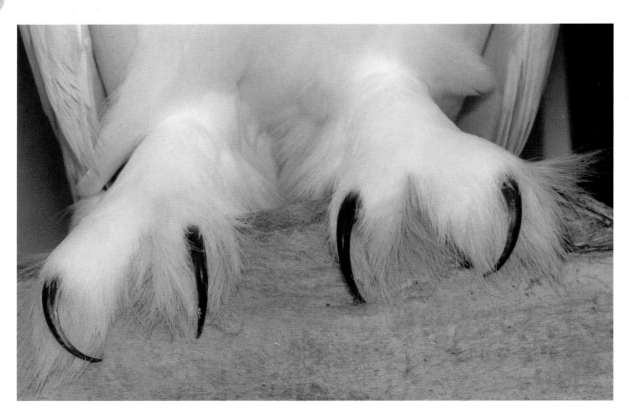

of each foot, so they can perch or grab prey with two toes forward and two backward. This rectangular pattern of the spread talons gives owls a considerable advantage when grasping and securing prey, especially prey concealed by snow or vegetation that they have located and pounced on using sound alone.

Many owls—but only a few other kinds of birds—have hairlike feathers covering their legs, feet, and toes. The toes of owls at northern and colder latitudes, such as the Snowy Owl, have densely feathered toes to help them conserve body heat in the Arctic. Conversely, owls living in more tropical habitats, such as the Bare-shanked Screech Owl found in Central America, have bare feet and toes.

Above: Owls use the middle talon, also known as the scraping claw, for cleaning their bills after eating. The feathery foot above belongs to a Tawny Owl.

Left: Owls suited to warmer climates, such as this Burrowing Owl, have bare feet and toes.

25

The Biology of Owls

There is simply no room in a book of this nature to provide a comprehensive account of all aspects of owl biology. Therefore, I offer some interesting and striking examples from some of the owl species covered by the scope of this book.

Predation

The evolutionary arms race between predator and prey has produced animals that seem to be perfectly designed for the habitats they live in and the challenges of life on earth. But it is important to remember that, when you look at nature, you see the survivors. Countless individuals run the gauntlet of natural selection generation after generation, and not all organisms survive to reproduce. Within the constraints of retaining the ability to fly, owls have been molded by the slowly changing abilities of the prey they seek. Likewise, their prey have evolved according to the diversity of predators that depend on them to survive. No better example of this is the differential ability of small mammals to evade capture by owls, as documented in a study in Nevada. Kangaroo rats are active at night in exposed areas of sand dune habitats, whereas three other species of mice avoided open habitats and stayed within clumps of protective vegetation. Long-eared owls ate far fewer kangaroo rats and more of the reclusive rodents. The explanation for this anomaly lies with the leaping ability and exceptional hearing of kangaroo rats. They possess enlarged parts of the brain and skull dedicated to hearing, allowing them to detect even the exceptionally quiet flight of attacking owls. Furthermore, their elongated hind legs enable them to leap up into the air 18 inches and land up to 12 inches from their launching spot, seconds before an approaching owl strikes. Owls may yet adapt over generations to come to routinely capture such elusive prey. The variation in both anatomy and behavior among owls and their prey is the raw material for such innovation. Only once in over twenty-five years of observing wild Great Gray Owls did I see one swooping low over a road trying to catch an exposed mouse crossing the highway. The mouse leapt up into the air just before the owl struck. To my amazement, the owl deftly reached out with one of its long legs and snatched the unfortunate airborne mouse in its talons while never even missing a wing beat.

In some cases prey species actually benefit from living and breeding

Opposite: The Western Screech Owl is especially active at dusk, when it will often catch its prey mid-flight.

Above: A Great Gray Owl silently swoops on its prey. It can extend its long legs to capture prey without missing a wing beat.

close to nesting owls in what may be best described as a kind of uneasy truce. Snow Geese and other bird species often initiate nests within 600 yards of active Snowy Owl nests in the Arctic tundra. Given that these other birds are known to be eaten by Snowy Owls, at first glance this appears to be a terrible idea. But in years when lemming species in the Arctic reach epidemic proportions these lemmings are the preferred prey of Snowy Owls intent on raising large broods. The owls perhaps benefit from the presence of the geese, which honk out an alarm at the first sight of predators such as the Arctic Fox. The owls then fly out and attack the approaching fox, often driving it away from the area. Researchers have documented that Snow Geese nesting near Snowy Owl nests often raise more young than those nesting farther away. For many birds, it seems that nesting near Snowy Owls is a worthwhile risk.

Occasionally the tables are turned, and the hunter becomes the hunted. Records of raptors killing and eating other raptors of the same or different species are interesting. It is hard to determine if such events are simply predation (many owls do eat other birds, after all) or a mechanism whereby the victor was eliminating the competition. One incident stands out in that it involves perhaps the only owl species that falconers have been able to train to regularly hunt other birds—the Northern Hawk Owl. An avid bird biologist recounted a fatal duel between a Northern Hawk Owl and a Northern Goshawk, a raptor that specializes in eating other birds. In early October he first observed some tiny Black-capped Chickadees harassing a Northern Hawk Owl perched in an older forestry cut over area. Then the goshawk flew in and pursued the hawk owl, which seemed to lack the escape maneuvers needed to evade capture. Instead the owl flew in short rising and twisting circles and the goshawk caught the hawk owl in a few short seconds. After waiting about half an hour, the curious biologist went closer to the site to have a look. The goshawk appeared to be annoyed to be thus disturbed as it was consuming the still-quivering owl's legs first.

Below: Many owls close their eyes' protective and translucent nictitating membranes just before striking their prey, like this Snowy Owl.

Breeding

All owls lay oval white eggs, and for many species the number of eggs they lay relates to the availability of food in the area around the nest site, which can vary considerably from year to year. In years when prey is scarce, resident owls will forego nesting while migratory owls will disperse and seek out prey-rich areas in which to breed. Recently I discovered another curious aspect of owl egg biology that I had never encountered before during my field research or when reviewing published scientific journals. A few years ago, I was studying a breeding pair of Northern Saw-whet Owls that had laid a very small clutch of only two eggs, or so I thought. These owls had used a wooden nest box in my yard site, and the female and male were first-time breeders. The first time I carefully opened the top of the nest box and peered in to see if it was occupied, the incubating female fiercely glared up at me, refusing to leave her clutch of eggs. I left her alone over the next few days until my curiosity got the best of me and I again opened the box.

I had to reach in at great risk to my ungloved hand and gently nudge the female to one side to count her clutch of three eggs. Northern Saw-whet

Opposite: The Great Gray Owl lays two to five eggs in late March through April. It uses old stick nests built by large hawks or ravens, as well as the rotted tops of broken trees.

Below: Barn owls usually lay a clutch of four to seven eggs, but when prey is abundant it can lay as many as fifteen eggs.

30

Owls can lay up to seven eggs, but young females breeding for the first time often lay smaller clutches. What was amazing was that while two of the eggs were of normal size, the third egg was about one-quarter the size of the others. Apparently, the laying of dwarf eggs has been recorded for other birds but not yet for owls. Researching this phenomenon, I learned that it is more common among first time breeding females than older females. The Saw-whet Owl pair raised two owlets and I was able to band the whole family, which dispersed later that fall. The dwarf egg never hatched.

Mate Choice

How males and females chose their mates is a fascinating field of research in any animal group, and owls are no exception. Seeking out a healthy mate is extremely important in the high-stakes game of sexual selection and the survival of the fittest. Less-romantic humans may exchange medical references or health assessments, but animals have no such recourse. Animals, including humans, have evolved the ability to detect signals of biological fitness in their potential mates that range from chemical cues to visual signs such as the symmetry of facial features or body parts. In birds, it is the plumage that often "makes the bird," so to speak. One example is the choosiness of male Barn Owls when picking from potential female mates based on the degree to which they are spotted. Males prefer more heavily spotted females. Research has shown that there is an energetic cost to having spots, and that spots are inherited traits. Apparently the young of females that are

Opposite: A prolonged courtship, which involves calling to one another, hopping from branch to branch, and wing displays like the one shown by the two Little Owls on the left, takes place before owls come together to mate. Mating takes place in late winter to spring.

Below: While owls lead fairly solitary lives outside of the breeding season, nesting pairs interact constantly to raise their young. Below are two Great Gray Owls protecting their nest.

heavily spotted are more resistant to a small bloodsucking fly that can reduce the quality and quantity of offspring. A heavily spotted female indicates to a choosy male that she can produce young with the genetic ability to resist the parasitic fly.

Bed and Breakfast—Owl Style

The Eastern Screech Owl is a generalist predator, eating a large variety of prey, including small snakes. Therefore it was quite a surprise for two biologists studying them in Texas to discover that not all prey that their study animals captured ended up as dinner! When cleaning out owl nest boxes after the breeding season, they discovered live Texas Blind Snakes among the nesting material. These small, sightless snakes grow up to 8 inches long and normally live under rocks and logs by day. At night they crawl out to hunt ant pupae, insect larvae, worms, and other invertebrates. How the live snakes got into nest boxes placed high up in trees was a mystery. This puzzle was solved when owls were seen to occasionally carry live blind snakes to their nest boxes. Owls usually kill their prey right after they capture them, and then deliver the dead animals to the nest. Why did

Below: Great Gray Owls live primarily off small rodents, with voles being their most important food source.

Left: A Spotted Eagle Owl with its prey. These owls prey on small mammals, birds, insects, frogs, and reptiles. They can swallow some large prey whole.

these owls not kill the snakes, and why did they allow them to live in their nests? It turns out that this arrangement is not that different from a bed-and-breakfast type of accommodation for the snakes.

Owls may not be the best housekeepers, but you have to admire their efforts. Breeding females often eat the feces and pellets (regurgitated, indigestible remains of prey) produced by their young, and then fly off to regurgitate the smelly mass far from the nest. This reduces the smell and likelihood of attracting mammalian predators to the nest. But the females seem to get overwhelmed by the task when their owlets get too large and "productive." Owl nests eventually accumulate significant amounts of debris consisting of leftover prey remains and plenty of owl droppings. This debris also attracts insects that lay their eggs in both prey remains and in nest material. Some of these guests are not welcome, as insect larvae can slow young owl growth by directly parasitizing them. Insect larvae also consume prey remains left or cached by the adults in the nest for the young to eat later. Ants can provide sanitation services to owl nests without negatively affecting the young owls, but some ant species consume both the stored prey items and owlets alike. So how do the snakes fit in?

The Texas-based biologists documented that young screech owls were

Right: Owls save considerable time by using other birds' discarded nests, tree or cliff cavities, man-made structures built especially for owls, as well as barns, houses, and derelict buildings. On the right, a Pygmy Owl looks up from her nest.

Opposite: Young of the Northern Hawk Owl hatch after up to thirty days incubation, and they usually leave the nest three weeks later. Adults feed their young for up to three months.

not harmed by the snakes. Rather, the owlets grew faster in nests with live snakes than in those without the insect larvae-eating serpents. This remarkable behavior reminds us that even the presumably instinctive act of killing captured prey can be altered or molded by natural selection to produce surprising beneficial results. What remains unknown is if snake-eating Elf or Whiskered Screech Owls also occasionally bring them to their nest sites alive. Ultimately, it would be interesting to know if Eastern Screech Owls are conscious of the consequences of their actions when carrying out this atypical behavior.

Owl Nesting Biology and Dispersal

With only one possible exception, owls do not build their own nests. They save considerable time and energy by using either the nests of other birds or natural structures, or by simply nesting in the underground burrows of fossorial mammals or in culverts and pipes, on the ground, in stick nests in trees, in tree or cliff cavities, in man-made structures built for owls or in barns, houses, or derelict buildings. Resident Burrowing Owls in Florida may be the only owl species that digs its own nest burrow. In the wild the male hunts for and feeds the female during courtship, while she incubates the eggs and broods the young until they can thermoregulate, and then, while she protects them from danger as they are developing and gaining their independence. In

captivity these roles tend to get mixed up and some captive males try to incubate, much to the dismay of their mates. A breeding pair usually cares for their young until the changing seasons affect their hormones and the plumage of the young changes such that the adults are stimulated to stop feeding them. Then the adults ignore them, disperse, migrate, or actively chase them out of their year-round home range. Documenting the home range and dispersal of owls is perhaps one of the fastest-growing aspects of owl research. This growth is fueled by the technological wizardry that has rapidly shrunk the electronic devices known as telemetry transmitters and the establishment of geosynchronized satellites in orbit around the earth, known as a global positioning system (GPS).

A Short-Eared Owl Gets a Platform Terminal Transmitter

Short-eared Owls have challenged the patience and ingenuity of many an owl biologist bent on studying this species' natural history to help conserve a shrinking population and manage its remaining habitat. Predicting when and where winter roosting or summer breeding colonies will be established can be like predicting the location of an electron in

Below: A satellite unit, called a Platform Terminal Transmitter, is fitted to a Short-Eared Owl. This technology helps scientists map their migration and dispersal patterns.

orbit around a nucleus. Once found, the owls need to be captured to mark or band them in order to learn more about their longevity and lifetime home ranges, and to determine if their migrations are truly nomadic or closer to a regular migration. Their reported tendency to travel nomadically over great distances means that recapturing marked individuals is unlikely to yield data or information. While impressive, the long-term band recovery information (spanning almost 100 years of effort) is very limited, yet it reveals that this species may exhibit a "leapfrog" migration pattern. This means that birds at the northern parts of their breeding range migrate farther south in winter than do birds breeding in more central areas. Better documentation of breeding dispersal is needed for this widespread threatened grassland owl. Advancements in solar-powered satellite technology have shrunk transmitter unit size to the point where even this medium-size owl can carry one harnessed to its back.

Below: Measuring the wing of a fledgling Burrowing Owl.

Left and opposite: The use of satellite technology has shown that Short-eared Owls nesting in Alaska and Alberta are nomadic migrants. They winter from Alberta to Texas, and then subsequently breed in wide-ranging areas such as Montana, Idaho, Alberta, and Saskatchewan.

These satellite units, called Platform Terminal Transmitters or PTTs, are not practical for nocturnal owl species that roost in dark nooks and crannies such as tree cavities or in trees in shadowy forests. If mounted on such species the unit is not exposed to the sunlight needed to recharge the battery. But Short-eared Owls live and roost in open, sunlit areas during the day. Scientists in different parts of North America are collaborating in marking Short-eared Owls with PTTs to help better map their migration and dispersal patterns. However, Short-eared Owls are notoriously difficult to capture—except as young birds in the nest—and these are too small to carry a PTT and harness. My wife and I set out to trap a Short-eared Owl for satellite marking not far from our home. After a few days of trying conventional owl trapping methods, we discovered an effective method. We used an imprinted, unreleasable Long-eared Owl (named Nemo) as a lure to get an aggressive territorial male Short-eared Owl close enough to catch it in flight with a handheld net gun powered by compressed air. We banded and marked the owl, and then excitedly shared the method with our colleagues. Alaskan biologists have now taken this method to the next level by net-gunning flying Short-eared Owls from helicopters in remote wilderness areas. So what did all these satellite-marked owls teach us? We now know that Short-eared Owls nesting in Alaska and Alberta are nomadic migrants, wintering from Alberta to Texas, and then subsequently breeding in wide-ranging areas such as Montana, Idaho, Alberta, and Saskatchewan. One owl marked in Saskatchewan flew a remarkable 621 miles to Minnesota in less than fourteen days. In contrast, Short-eared Owls in eastern North America exhibit a more typical migration pattern. Owls

marked in winter in New York and southern Ontario ended up breeding in Labrador and northern Quebec, and then returned to the same winter roosts where they were marked the previous year.

Perhaps the most compelling example of this owl's remarkable migratory capacity comes from one person's anecdotal observation not involving high-tech gadgetry. On Monday, October 13, 2008, Kelly Curtis emailed me that she had encountered an owl while on a ship in the middle of the North Pacific Ocean (41N 143W). The owl had apparently been following the ship for some time. I didn't know of any seagoing owls and had to ask various questions to help identify it.

Kelly and I exchanged details about the owl she was able to repeatedly observe, and we concluded that it was a Short-eared Owl. I plotted Kelly's Pacific Ocean coordinate on Google Earth and it was a staggering 900 miles from the west coast of North America. Some owls are capable of long flights over water, and the Short-eared Owl is clearly one of them. It has even established itself in Florida from a population in the Greater Antilles, in the Galápagos, and on other islands.

Distribution and Conservation

Owls, like humans, are found in almost all regions of the earth except some remote islands, most of Greenland, and Antarctica. Fewer than five owl species live in northern Canada's Arctic and subarctic regions, whereas five to ten species can be found over the vast majority of North and Central America. Owl biodiversity hot spots, where ten to fifteen owl species coexist, are found in limited parts of southwestern Canada and the western United States, and in about a third of Central America. Given that many owls have large home ranges and are excellent indicators of an ecosystem's health, a focused conservation effort on their behalf can provide a means to achieve wider ecosystem conservation objectives.

The International Union for Conservation of Nature (IUCN) assesses the conservation status of wildlife species into categories ranging from least concern to extinct using standard criteria such as taxonomic status, range or distribution size and trend, population size and trend, and threats. The IUCN status of owl species is provided in the following species chapters. Using species status information provides a means by which the geographic patterns and changes in owl species diversity over time can be related to changes in climate and human populations. They can also identify priority geographic conservation hot spots, where limited conservation funds and resources can be directed.

Opposite: Compared to other birds, a slightly higher proportion of the world's owls are considered endangered or vulnerable at the global scale. This may be because most owls, like the Great Gray Owl on the left, depend on forested habitats, especially those with mature trees that provide nest sites including cavities.

43

Above: A Northern Hawk Owl being weighed before banding and release.

Compared to all birds, a slightly higher proportion of owls are considered endangered or vulnerable at the global scale. This may be because most owls depend on forested habitats, especially those with mature trees that provide nesting cavities. The leading cause of species endangerment is habitat loss, destruction, or degradation. The clearing of forested habitats and the conversion of natural grasslands and wetlands to make way for agriculture and urbanization has accelerated dramatically along with human population growth. Both forest-dwelling owls and open country species like the Short-eared Owl and many Barn Owl species have experienced population and distribution declines as a result. Other direct threats to owls include the use of pesticides to control insects and rodents, and collisions with vehicles and wires. All these threats have impacted local populations of widespread species. Climate change and its impacts on habitats have been identified as a significant new and additional threat to owl species that have restricted distributions, such as island-dwelling owls or owls that are found in isolated montane regions.

You can help owls in many ways. Volunteers in the thousands help count birds, including owls, in general or specialized bird surveys, helping to document distributions, habitat use, and population trends. Some of the threats facing owls can be mitigated locally through the development of recovery strategies and the implementation of recovery or management action plans. The provision of nest boxes or artificial nesting structures is a labor-intensive and short-term solution that has maintained or restored local owl populations. The protection and conservation of significant remaining habitats is a long-term and ultimately more efficient conservation strategy. Wildlife-related ecotourism can provide local people and communities with alternative means to earn a living off of intact ecosystems in a sustainable manner. Perhaps the best long-term solution to maintaining owl and other wildlife populations will be the management of our own population numbers to a reasonable level.

The coexistence of owls and people across most of the globe and over thousands of years means that different cultures have had countless opportunities to know and admire them or, in some cases, despise them due to their association with the nighttime and dark places. The rich and diverse cultural, spiritual, and scientific relationship between owls and humans has been the focus of many books and articles. Among the most

Below: A Barred Owl is released back into the wild after treatment at a bird sanctuary in New Jersey.

45

bizarre are the uses of owl eggs or body parts as traditional medicines to cure hangovers, thinning hair, epilepsy, influenza, and many other ailments. However, humans have likely benefited more from live owls in the wild, for it is there that they consume a large number of insects, rodents, and other animals that we often consider pests. Our continued coexistence on earth will depend on the extent to which we are willing to share the planet's natural resources with owls and other species.

Below: A Snowy Owl in flight over the Alberta prairies. Fewer than five owl species live in northern Canada's Arctic and subarctic regions.

Note on Text and Maps

The owl species listed in this book include all forty-six species found in North and Central America. The order of the owl species follows that of international standardized lists as presented in the 2012 and 2009 *Owls of the World* reference books listed in the bibliography. The owl range maps that accompany each species are adapted from recent references listed in the bibliography. They depict the distribution of owls as accurately as possible as small scale maps allow. Green shows the year-round range of resident owl species. For migratory species, yellow shows their summer range and purple shows their winter range. Arrows show either nomadic or irruptive movements or point out small islands that are part of the distribution. Question marks indicate parts of the range that are uncertain at this time.

Below: The Great Horned Owl has the most extensive distribution in North America.

Common Barn Owl

Tyto alba

This medium-size charismatic nocturnal raptor has a wingspan of 35–43 inches, with males slightly lighter and smaller on average. It has a pale, usually bright white, heart-shaped face with a prominent ridge of feathers above the ivory bill and between small, blackish eyes. This, combined with its lack of ear tufts, makes it unique in appearance compared to all other North American owl species—it looks similar only to other species of the genus *Tyto* that are found elsewhere. It is also distinguished from other owls of North America by its exceptionally buoyant flight when its relatively long wings, dangling long-feathered legs, and a short, square-ended tail are readily apparent. Its head and upper body plumage, including the forehead and back, have elegant black and white specks but otherwise can vary from ash-gray to yellowish-brown. The underparts are white, occasionally with a few black flecks. The lower legs are lightly feathered and the feet are brownish to yellowish-white. Females and juveniles are typically more heavily spotted than males.

It was described first in 1769 by Italian biologist Giovanni Scopoli. Its scientific species name *alba* describes its white color. The wings and tail are light brown with dark bands. Over thirty subspecies have been described worldwide. It is sometimes recognized as a separate species, the American Barn Owl (*Tyto furcata*) in North America with up to five subspecies. The taxonomy of *Tyto* is still subject to debate and needs clarification. Other informal common names include the Monkey-faced, Rat, Death, and Hobgoblin Owl.

A typical call of the male Barn Owl is a frightening, harsh or rough scream, screech, or chatter uttered at variable intervals near the female or its nest site. Females will also occasionally give a version of this call. More intimate twittering sounds are given by males and females as part of pair formation, such as when males are transferring prey to their mates. Hungry young and food-demanding females will give a "snoring" call, and females feeding owlets will "twitter." Males and females will also exchange a

Total Length
   12.5–15.5 inches
Wing Chord (unflattened)
   11.4–14.1 inches
Tail 4.4–6 inches
Weight 13.7–20 ounces

purring call during courtship. Other sounds noted include a low croaking sound and a raspy noise mixed with hissing and bill-snapping when owls are surprised at close quarters.

The Barn Owl is one of the most widely dispersed of all the owls, being found on every continent except Antarctica. In South America, it's found on oceanic islands like the Galápagos, and it is also found in Eurasia, most of Africa, India, parts of the Malaysian archipelago, and Australia, including Tasmania. In North America it is found mainly in the northern states into some adjacent parts of Canada (British Columbia and southern Ontario), and south through Mexico and Central America. It was introduced to Hawaii in 1958. It seems to avoid areas with snow cover that persists for more than a month or so; hence, its range may be expanding northward as global climate change continues to warm the planet. While adults tend to be year-round residents, their young are known to disperse up to 1,000 miles in search of breeding sites.

The Barn Owl may be seen hunting in the early evening, but it is usually nocturnal. Nonetheless, it can occasionally be seen flying in daylight, perhaps when an individual is displaced from its day roost by a disturbance, or driven to this atypical behavior by the hunger cries of its young. It flies quietly, often gliding for long distances interrupted by a brief series of wing beats. Daytime roosts are mainly located in nests or other cavities, in caves, or in the dark corners of barns, sheds, and abandoned derelict buildings. Some owls will get used to sleeping in human-occupied structures, too. Even though pairs may continue to roost together throughout the year, each spring they reaffirm their bond with an elaborate aerial courtship. The Barn Owl either hunts from low perches, often fence posts, or while flying low over open weedy fields and other grassland or marshy habitats.

Most juvenile Barn Owls die within a year, and those that survive usually only live for one to two years. In one study, the average life span was 1.7 years. However, some individuals have lived for over twenty-nine years in the wild, and a female Barn Owl in England bred and kept in captivity lived for twenty-five years. Another captive barn owl reportedly lived for thirty-four years.

The Barn Owl captures a great variety of animals using its powerful talons, including insects, amphibians, small reptiles, and birds, but mainly takes small terrestrial mammals such as voles, shrews, mice, and rats. It can even catch bats in flight. Its ability to locate concealed prey using sound in near-dark conditions is legendary.

It lives either in pairs that appear to mate for life, or as single birds.

Occasionally, especially when prey is abundant, a male will nest with two females simultaneously. Females normally lay a clutch of four to seven eggs, but when prey is abundant as many as fifteen eggs can be laid. Most natural nests are in tree cavities up to sixty-six feet aboveground, but they will also readily use sheltered sites in old houses, barns, and even caves and well shafts. Incubation lasts about thirty-two days, owlets are brooded for two weeks, and young leave the nest when fifty to fifty-five days old. Juveniles disperse within weeks and can breed when only ten months old. Some pairs in southern latitudes can nest as many as three times a year, especially when mice, voles, and rats are plentiful. The Barn Owl prefers mainly open grasslands with scattered trees near towns and villages, open woodland, marshland, and peats. Home range estimates are variable, ranging from 726 acres in Virginia, 912 acres in Texas, 761 acres in Scotland, and more than 1,853 acres in France.

Like most species, habitat loss threatens local populations of this otherwise common species. Secondary poisoning from eating rodents killed by rodenticides and pesticides has been linked to localized Barn Owl deaths. The construction and installation of artificial nest boxes has helped to offset the loss of nest sites in old barns and other buildings replaced by modern structures. Barn Owls are found dead from vehicle collisions more often in winter as they tend to hunt along busy roads, especially where road right-of-ways offer the only foraging habitat for dispersing young owls. Expanding highway and road networks, and increased vehicle traffic, have increased rates of roadkill mortality. Natural episodes of local mortality are linked to periodic harshly cold and snowy winters in temperate climates. The Barn Owl does not have the ability to store sufficient fat reserves to tolerate severe weather, causing entire populations in these climates to starve and perish. Despite such factors, this species remains abundant and widespread across the world, such that it is still listed as least concern (IUCN). The Barn Owl has been assessed as endangered in eastern Canada owing to a very small population in this region, and its North American population is declining with the continued loss of suitable grassland ecosystems. Despite all the threats facing this species, its population can rebound quickly during peak prey years.

Flammulated Owl

Psiloscops flammeolus

Total Length

  6–6.7 inches

Wing Chord (unflattened)

  5–5.9 inches

Tail 2.3–2.7 inches

Weight 1.6–2.2 ounces

The Flammulated Owl has short, usually flattened ear tufts on an angular head; dark brown eyes; and a gray-brown bill within an incomplete gray to rusty-brown and dark-rimmed facial disk. Its light gray bill has a lighter tip. Both the short tail and long, gray-brown, pointed wings have dark and light colored bars. A rusty orange-brown stripe is visible at the base of its upper wings. Its body feathers range from gray to red, with dark crossbars and shaft streaks giving it a mottled appearance. Gray-brown feathers cover its legs to the base of its likewise colored toes. In the northern parts of its range, where Douglas firs are dominant, the gray color phase predominates. In southern areas, where it uses pine forests, the red phase is more prevalent.

It was first described in 1852 by German scientist Johannes Kaup, and its scientific species name describes its flamelike coloration. Three subspecies (*P. f. flammeolus, P. f. idahoensis,* and *P. f. rarus*) are recognized by some authorities. DNA evidence has revealed that the Flammulated Owl is not related to American Screech Owls (*Megascops*) nor to Old World Scops Owls (*Otus*), and therefore it has been placed in the oldest generic name for this species, *Psiloscops*. Other common names used over time include the Flammulated Screech or Flammulated Scops Owl, and the Dwarf Owl.

This tiny owl has a hoarse, low frequency song comprised of "woop" notes that is reminiscent of a much larger owl. It can produce this low-pitched song due to a specialized throat structure. Early in the breeding season it sings its flat, short, ventriloquistic hoots, repeated at two- to three-second intervals, for hours on end. It also utters a two-note "boo-boot" call at one-and-a-half-second intervals. Its alarm call is described as a kittenlike "meow."

The Flammulated Owl is found in El Salvador, Guatemala, and Mexico, and north along the Rocky Mountains in the United States to British

Columbia. There is not much known about the winter distribution, habitat use, and diet of this owl. Also unknown is the extent to which populations in Mexico migrate. In contrast, individuals of northern breeding populations need to relocate or migrate considerable distances at night in order to find wintering habitats with a sufficient supply of insect prey.

It is active at night, especially at dusk, and occasionally through to dawn. Daytime roosts are typically well hidden, or close to tree trunks, where its plumage helps camouflage it as a broken branch. Prey are captured either in flight, off of foliage or branches, or on the ground.

This species is known to have lived as long as thirteen years in the wild and for fourteen years in captivity.

Insects form the main part of its diet, including grasshoppers, crickets, and caterpillars, but especially moths and beetles. Other invertebrates eaten include spiders, centipedes, and scorpions.

While single pairs are found in some areas, other breeding locations have clusters of breeding pairs with overlapping territories, suggesting that this species is somewhat colonial, resulting in large areas of otherwise apparently suitable breeding habitats remaining unoccupied between breeding locations. Former Pileated Woodpecker or Northern Flicker nest cavities are used by the Flammulated Owl for nesting, but it will also breed in man-made nest boxes. It typically lays two to three egg clutches, but occasionally up to four white eggs are found. Females incubate the eggs for up to twenty-eight days. Both adults feed their young in the nest for three to five weeks, and for up to another five weeks after the owlets leave the nest.

At the northern reaches of its range it uses dry Douglas fir forests. Elsewhere, it's mainly found in mature ponderosa and yellow pine stands, sometimes mixed with aspen or oak trees, where nest structures, shelter from predators, and its food supply of moths and beetles are more abundant. Such forests typically have trees of various sizes with a diverse understory of brush, shrubs, and grasses, and it ranges from elevations of 1,300 to 9,840 feet. Average home range estimates from Colorado and Oregon were similar at thirty-six and thirty-nine acres, respectively. Its home range size decreased over the breeding season through incubation and was as small as nine acres during the fledgling period.

While the Flammulated Owl population is thought to be declining owing to ongoing harvesting of pine and fir trees within its forest habitat, the decline is slow enough not to trigger a high-priority IUCN conservation status assessment. It was deemed to be rare until survey techniques using its song, played back to solicit responses from territorial males, resulted in increased population estimates. Now it is thought to be one of the most common owls of mountain pine forests in the western United States and Mexico. Some concern for its long-term conservation status remains, however, as it has small clutch sizes and is limited to breeding in commercially important forests, which are subject to extensive fragmentation.

Western Screech Owl

Megascops kennicottii

Total Length 7.5–10 inches

Wing Chord (unflattened)
5.6–7.5 inches

Tail 2.8–3.9 inches

Weight 3.2–8.8 ounces

This small owl has a black or gray bill with prominent, stiff rictal bristles (feathers) at its base; feathered ear tufts; and yellow eyes set in a dark-rimmed facial disk. Like other *Megascops* owls, it exhibits considerable color variation across its range, including the relatively rare brownish-red morph in Pacific Northwest coastal areas, pale gray in southern desert ecosystems, and brownish-gray elsewhere. Its facial disk likewise varies, ranging from brownish-white with brown-gray mottling to buff-cinnamon. Its size and weight also varies across its distribution, with northern individuals weighing as much as a third less than heavier southern birds. Its bill color, distinct calls, fine dark horizontal bars at right angles to bold feather shaft streaks on the ventral area, and parallel dark streaks on upper body feathers help distinguish it from its eastern cousin. Its plumage gives it the appearance of rough tree bark. The wings and tail are barred, and there is a fine mottling on its legs. Juveniles have more heavily marked stripes and bars and more white-tipped feathers, but otherwise are similar in appearance to adults.

It was first described by Daniel Elliot in 1867 and was named to recognize famed explorer and naturalist Robert Kennicott, who died in 1866. Its original common name was Kennicott's Owl, but it has also been informally called the Little Cat Owl and the Coastal Screech Owl. Formerly a subspecies of the similar Eastern Screech

Owl, the Western Screech Owl has been further split into three species: *M. kennicottii, M. seductus,* and *M. cooperi.* It has been moved from the genus *Otus* to *Megascops.*

"A bouncing ball coming to a rest" is the common description of this owl's distinct song, which consists of bouts of five to fifteen steady-pitched, whistled hollow "hoo" notes that start slow and speed up to a trill at the end of the calling bout. Other songs include a fast double trill, a softer contact or greeting "cr-r-oo-oo-oo-oo" call, and a terse, barking alarm call.

Its distribution includes northern Sinaloa through Chihuahua and Coahuila of the Mexican highlands, north to Baja California and western Texas, western Oklahoma, Colorado, northwestern Wyoming, western Montana, northern Idaho, and southeastern Alaska, and coastal and southern British Columbia. This owl may be expanding its range east along riparian areas in Colorado and Texas, and the Great Plains north to Saskatchewan. While this owl is essentially a year-round resident, or nonmigratory, its young disperse up to 185 miles starting in midsummer

when they gain their independence. It is a relatively common owl at lower elevations in western North America. Its range overlaps with the Whiskered Screech Owl in southern Arizona and Mexico, and with the Eastern Screech Owl in eastern Colorado and southern Texas.

It is primarily nocturnal, and is especially active at dusk. By day it perches at concealed roost sites, such as tree cavities, thick vegetation, or up tight against a tree trunk. It sits upright with erect ear tufts and loose, relaxed plumage that hides its legs and yellow-toed feet, giving it a chunky look. This appearance changes when it feels threatened—it then lengthens its body and compresses its feathers, such that it resembles a broken branch. If threatened at close range or when it thinks it has been detected, it may silently fly away, flapping its wings about five times per second, sometimes in an erratic, batlike fashion through forested habitat. It looks stout in flight due to its tucked-in head and broad wings. It stalks its prey from branches and other perches in forests and woodland edges near meadows and wetlands, from which it catches prey in flight or by pouncing on it on the ground.

Like many small owls, it falls prey to many predators, including crows, the Northern Goshawk, and other diurnal birds of prey, and at least six larger owl species such as the Long-eared Owl. Snakes and mammals, including squirrels, mink, weasels, raccoons, and skunks, also kill and eat it. While one individual managed to live up to twelve years and eleven months in the wild, most only live for just under two years before they perish. The oldest known captive bird lived for nineteen years.

Mice, voles, rats, and other small mammals, birds, and large insects such as grasshoppers, locusts, beetles, moths, and butterflies form the bulk of its diverse diet. It also eats small fish, salamanders, frogs, reptiles, bats, snails, slugs, scorpions, crayfish, and worms.

A breeding pair of Western Screech Owls will renew their pair bond by singing together, perching closer, and preening each other, and by the male feeding the female before copulating. Morphs of different colors will interbreed. Western Screech Owl clutches are typically three to seven eggs laid in tree cavities such as old woodpecker nests six to fifty feet aboveground, or in artificial nest boxes in forest stands. Larger clutches are found in the northeastern parts of its range. A male and female can remain paired for many years and may reuse a nest site in successive years. If a nest is predated early in the breeding season, the pair may nest there again that year. The male feeds its mate while she incubates the eggs for about twenty-six days, and while she broods the young, which fledge when thirty-five days old; they disperse in the fall. Both sexes will aggressively defend their young from large predators, including people.

Common features of the diverse habitat types used by the Western Screech Owl across its range include suitable nest tree cavities and plentiful prey populations that are accessible such as in open forests, especially

lowland riparian forests. Typical nest trees include deciduous species such as junipers, oaks, willows, cottonwoods, sycamores, and maples. Some desert populations nest in saguaro and other large cacti; elsewhere, coniferous nest tree species include firs and junipers. It also avoids habitats where its main predators, such as the Great Horned Owl, exist. Habitat types include desert cacti groves, mesquite and Joshua tree stands, oak ravines, and pine and pinyon-juniper forests in the south

to moist western red cedar, Sitka spruce, and western hemlock forests adjacent to lakes, rivers, and open areas in the north. At the northern parts of its range it avoids higher elevations, which is perhaps tied to the distribution of its preferred deciduous forest habitat. It is found frequently in riparian woodlands but also in a variety of treed and forested habitats. Home ranges can be up to 150 acres, and are occupied by breeding pairs year-round. A male's territorial song can be heard year-round, but it only defends a small area around the nest site (or sites) aggressively. In some parts of its range there is considerable overlap in the home ranges of adjacent pairs, especially in desert habitats where nests can be as close as 165 feet apart.

Over the last forty years in North America, it has experienced a large and significant decrease, but this decline has not yet triggered concern at the global level. In Canada it is found only in British Columbia, where it has recently been assessed as threatened due to serious population declines, including its near disappearance in the southern part of its Canadian range over the last ten to fifteen years. While it remains locally abundant in many areas, habitat loss due to cutting of riparian forests, clear-cut timber harvesting, and housing developments are possible causes of such overall declines. Threats that can cause local extirpations include the removal of snags or dead trees used as nest sites and roosts, susceptibility to pesticide-induced eggshell thinning, and additional predation from newly established populations of Barred Owls. Some populations persist in forested suburban habitats and protected city parks, and they will breed in man-made nest boxes.

Eastern Screech Owl

Megascops asio

Total Length

7.1–9.1 inches

Wing Chord (unflattened)

5.7–6.9 inches

Tail 2.4–3.9 inches

Weight 4.4–8.8 ounces

This small owl with prominent ear tufts has a continuum of color phases, with gray and cinnamon-red morphs at either extreme. Some brownish individuals fall within the gradient and are present in most populations. The ratio of color morphs is thought to vary across its range with humidity and temperature, with reddish owls comprising about a third of the entire population. The red phase is less frequent and tolerant of cold climates in more northern latitudes, more common at the eastern edge of the range, and absent from parts of southern Texas. Its black-bordered whitish or reddish mottled facial disk contains lemon-yellow eyes that reportedly darken with age, and a light greenish-yellow bill. It is distinguished from the Western Screech Owl by its plumage, bill color, and calls, but they coexist only in southern Texas and eastern Colorado. Its underside has feathers with shaft streaks and horizontal bars that create an anchorlike pattern. The streaks on its upper body feathers flare out sideways. Its wings and tail are barred.

It was first described by the famous Swedish naturalist Carolus Linnaeus in 1758. In 2003 it was moved from the genus *Otus* into the genus *Megascops*. At least six subspecies are recognized, including *M. a. asio, M. a. floridanus, M. a. hasbroucki, M. a. maxwelliae, M. a. mccallii,* and *M. a. naevius*. Its species name, *asio*, is Latin for "horned owl," and some of its informal common names include the Ghost Owl, Spirit Owl, and Little-eared Owl.

This owl gives a variety of defensive rasps, chuckles, hoots, screeches, and barks, including a descending horselike whinny uttered during the breeding season. Its characteristic territorial song is monotonous, or sometimes a descending two- to three-second-long trill consisting of thirty-five or so notes, reminiscent of a toad. Females have higher-pitched calls than males, and breeding pairs sometimes sing together in duets. Hungry young out of the nest demand food with a rough "keeeerr-r-r."

Its distribution includes northeastern Mexico, along the Gulf of Mexico and Florida, in the eastern United States to eastern Montana, and north to Saskatchewan, Manitoba, Ontario, and Quebec. This territorial owl remains

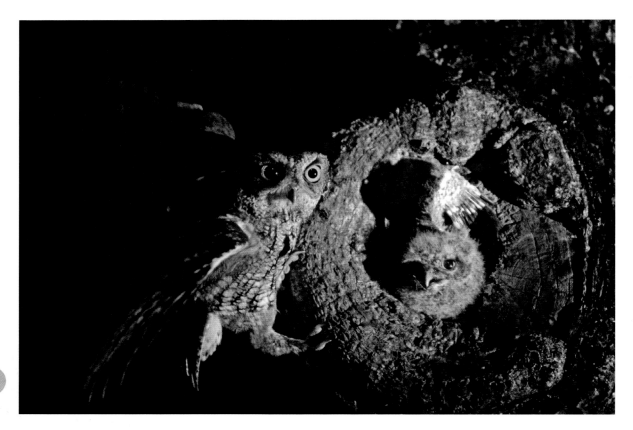

on its home range year-round. Young owls disperse as far as ten miles from their parents' breeding territory in autumn when twelve to fourteen weeks old.

It is mainly active and hunts at night, starting at dusk. It rarely glides or hovers; rather, its flight consists of regular but fast flapping of its broad wings at five wing beats per second. It is quite adept at navigating through forested habitats. It is stocky-looking both when flying and at rest, roosting within thick foliage, cavities, crevices in old buildings, or against tree trunks. When threats are detected it stretches itself tall and appears thinner, often partially closing its eyes and bringing a wrist up to its chin. They are adaptable hunters and can catch prey in flight, on branches, and on the ground. It hunts from perches in, or adjacent to, open areas such as lawns, wetlands, fields, and open forest understories.

The average Eastern Screech Owl lives for only two to three years, but one wild owl lived to be twenty years and eight months old. This was just slightly older than the longevity record of twenty years in captivity. Each year about 70 percent of the juveniles and 30 percent of adults perish, with some being killed and eaten by other owl species, such as the Barred Owl, or mammals like raccoons and weasels. Some young have even choked to death while eating prey.

Terrestrial and aquatic invertebrates such as earthworms, snails, worms, scorpions, centipedes, crayfish, spiders, and a great variety of insects comprise much of its diet in summer months in northern parts of its range, and year-round elsewhere. Ever opportunistic, it will also capture and consume small fish, amphibians, reptiles, and birds such as songbirds, grouse, doves, and quail. Mammals eaten include shrews, moles, voles, mice, rats, chipmunks, squirrels, and bats. A thirty-year study in Texas showed that more birds were consumed in suburban habitats where the concentrations of bird feeders and birdbaths created a stable food source.

It lays up to six white eggs as early as mid-March to mid-May, but its usual clutch size is three to four. Breeding pairs, which can consist of morphs of mixed colors, typically remain together; however, mates are replaced if one dies or disappears. Males perform complex courtship behaviors such as singing, head and body gyrations, bobbing, bill-touching, and mutual preening. Nests are usually in deciduous tree cavities, often old Pileated Woodpecker and Northern Flicker nest sites, or in artificial nest boxes in forested areas, or even crevices in old buildings. Nest sites are

sometimes reused if not predated. Eggs are incubated for thirty days, and the female broods the young until they are able to thermoregulate—or generate their own heat from metabolism—at about eleven to fourteen days. Adults feed their rapidly growing young for about thirty days. One of their nicknames, "the feathered wildcat," undoubtedly arose from the often extremely aggressive response of breeding adults to animals that venture too close to their recently fledged young. They have been known to strike people's heads, sometimes drawing blood, when the humans walk unsuspectingly near fledged owls on the ground, or on low perches. Once young owls are able to fly or climb up to high perches, the assaults on people and their pets cease.

Habitats used by this owl include lower-elevation riparian forests, southern pine forests, southwestern oak-juniper, subtropical thorn woodland, northern and tropical deciduous and mixed forests, and occasionally boreal and montane coniferous forests, up to 4,900 feet in elevation. Both man-made and natural treed habitats are used. This owl appears to avoid areas with breeding Great Horned Owls, which in turn tend to select habitats with low human populations. It is unclear if this is the reason that Eastern Screech Owl densities increase in proportion to human populations in urban areas. Suburban and urban habitats are also warmer than rural areas. This may be the reason that breeding Eastern Screech Owls studied for three decades in Texas nested earlier and produced more owlets in suburban versus rural habitats. Nests can be as close as 164 feet because males aggressively defend only small areas near their nest sites. Rural breeding territories in wooded habitats are as large as seventy-five acres, whereas in forested urban areas territories range from ten to fifteen acres. Some estimates of undefended home ranges are as big as 200 acres.

The IUCN has given the Eastern Screech Owl a least concern status due to its large distribution and an estimated population of over 10,000 individuals. Urban and suburban treed habitats support healthy populations of this owl even at the extremes of its North American distribution. Short-term local studies have concluded that populations were in decline, but these were in error because the Eastern Screech Owl undergoes four- to ten-year population cycles. Longer-term and larger-scale monitoring efforts, such as the Breeding Bird Survey and the Christmas Bird Count, have documented significant population increases over the last forty years, allowing a better assessment of its conservation status.

Oaxaca Screech Owl

Megascops lambi

This owl has prominent ear tufts and yellow eyes set in a gray facial disk with a dark rim. Its bill is yellow-tipped, but mainly brown to olive-green, and it appears to have only one color phase. It was first described in 1959 from a specimen in Oaxaca, Mexico, and was formerly considered a subspecies of the Eastern Screech Owl. More research is needed to review and clarify the taxonomy of this group of owls. Its distribution overlaps with that of the Pacific Screech Owl, but owls are most often heard before they are seen, and knowledge of—or access to—recordings of owl songs and calls will distinguish it from this and other species. This owl derives its name from its restricted distribution in southwestern Mexico along the Pacific coast in the biologically diverse state of Oaxaca. It is likely a year-round resident.

Its primary song has been described as a guttural and gruff grunting trill, followed by a series of short, abrupt notes: "croarrr-gogogogogogok." Other song elements include a horselike whinny reminiscent of that of the Eastern Screech Owl. Both the female and male sing, with the female's notes distinctly higher-pitched. It is active from dusk through the night to dawn. Daytime roosts are typically perches hidden by vegetation or inside trees, plants, and other cavities. It eats insects and other invertebrates, as well as small vertebrates.

There is one report of a nest in May containing one egg and two owlets, suggesting that young likely fledge in May and perhaps into June.

The habitat it occupies ranges from sea level up to 3,300 feet, including coastal swamps and mangroves adjacent to thorn woodlands, with palms and cacti present. It has a restricted range on the Pacific slope and therefore may be a species of conservation concern. This species is still considered by many to be a subspecies of the Pacific Screech Owl, which is assessed as least concern. However, both the Pacific and Oaxaca Screech Owls require detailed study, if for no other reason than to properly assess their uncertain conservation status.

Total Length
7.9–8.7 inches

Wing Chord (unflattened)
5.8–6.5 inches

Tail 3–3.3 inches

Weight 4.1–4.6 ounces

Pacific Screech Owl

Megascops cooperi

Total Length
7.9–10.2 inches

Wing Chord (unflattened)
6.4–7.2 inches

Tail 3.1–3.5 inches

Weight 5.1–6 ounces

This fairly big screech owl has yellow eyes and a greenish bill set in a pale gray facial disk with a distinct dark edge. There is dark barring on the ear tufts and on the top of its head. Only one brownish-gray color morph exists. It was originally described by Robert Ridgway in 1878. In 1998 it was elevated from a subspecies of the Western Screech Owl to full species status. The taxonomic status of this poorly known owl would certainly benefit from additional molecular and biological research. The male's main song has not been described, but both sexes utter a "woof" note to keep in touch. Males and females sing together in what is described as a slow staccato "gogogogogo" that starts out as a fast trill of guttural "grurrr" notes, a sequence that is repeated at intervals separated by several seconds. The female's version of this song is higher-pitched than that of her mate.

The Pacific Screech Owl is thought to be a year-round resident along the southern Pacific coast of Mexico to Costa Rica. It is active from dusk through to dawn. Daytime roosts are perches in thick vegetation, or in trees and other cavities. While it can catch insect prey in flight, it mainly hunts from perches in areas where prey are vulnerable to capture, such as along the edges of forest openings. It eats scorpions, katydids, moths, beetles, other invertebrates, and likely small vertebrates, including rodents.

Three to five eggs are laid in tree cavities, probably mainly created by woodpeckers. It is occasionally found in low scrubby and mangrove habitats, including swampy forests from sea level to 3,300 feet elevation. More typical habitats used include arid to semiarid forests with open areas adjacent to lakes, but with palms, trees, giant cacti, shrubs, and secondary growth present. Current Costa Rican national parks where it can be found include Palo Verde, Barra Honda, and Santa Rosa. While less than 50,000 individuals are estimated to live in its entire global range, there is no actual information available on its population numbers or trends. Its formal conservation status is least concern.

Whiskered Screech Owl

Megascops trichopsis

Total Length

6.3–7.5 inches

Wing Chord (unflattened)

5.2–6.3 inches

Tail 2.4–3.1 inches

Weight 2.5–4.3 ounces

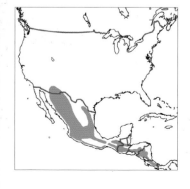

Numerous long, hairlike "whiskers" give this small owl its name. These modified feather structures are called rictal bristles and border its face and the pale yellow-grayish, sometimes greenish bill, and are especially prominent on the upper facial disk. Its yellow eyes are set in a dark facial disk and its head sports modest feathered ear tufts. Its color ranges from reddish in the south to light gray in the north. It was first described in 1832 from a specimen collected in Mexico.

Its call is a slow series of evenly spaced, monotonous whistles that vary in length, and which have been described as being similar to Morse code. It ranges from southwestern Arizona and southeastern New Mexico south through the Sierra Madre Occidental, and along mountain ranges to Nicaragua. The Whiskered Screech Owl may be a year-round resident. It is nocturnal, but is likely active at dawn and dusk as well. It catches mostly insects, but also enjoys small amphibians, reptiles, birds, and mammals.

Typical of the screech owls, it lays three to four eggs in former woodpecker nests or other natural tree cavities. It is found mainly at elevations ranging from 4,900 to 8,200 feet above sea level, perhaps reducing competition with the lower-elevation habitat of the Western Screech Owl, and sometimes higher-elevation haunts of the Flammulated Owl. While it is often found roosting in coffee plantations, its natural habitats include dense mountainside stands of mixed oak, pine, and sycamore forests, and also in canyons and riparian areas. Other birds, especially owls, are excluded from its aggressively defended nesting and hunting territory.

It has a relatively large distribution and its population is estimated to be greater than 10,000 adults. It appears to be increasing based on standardized breeding bird surveys and Christmas Bird Count data. It seems to remain locally abundant despite intense habitat changes in parts of its range caused by human intrusion. While its official conservation status is least concern, efforts to conserve or protect representative dense montane forests are still warranted in order to study its ecology in its natural habitat.

Bearded Screech Owl
Megascops barbarus

This relatively small screech owl has yellow eyes, speckled white eyebrows, and a greenish bill within a pale, brown-gray facial disk rimmed in dark brown. The ear tufts are so short that they often go undetected. It has a red and gray color phase. The folded wing tips extend past its short tail. The Bearded Screech Owl was first described in 1868 based on a specimen from Santa Barbara, Guatemala. It is sometimes called the Mustached Screech Owl.

The male's main song is a fast, cricketlike, three- to five-second trill depicted as "treerrrrrrrrrt" that gets louder before it stops altogether. Several seconds pass between repeated trills. The larger female has a higher-pitched version of this song and also utters gentler "dewd" notes in response to a singing male. It sings from within the forest canopy and is therefore hard to see.

It is found from central Guatemala to Chiapas, Mexico, and north to the highlands south of the Mexican isthmus. This year-round resident does not migrate, but young owls likely disperse over short distances when displaced by their parents and as they seek out their own home range. The Bearded Screech Owl's nocturnal habits often deter the efforts of those trying to locate this elusive species. The oldest known wild Bearded Screech Owl was a banded female that was at least four years old when recaptured.

The Bearded Screech Owl specializes in eating invertebrates such as beetles, crickets, moths, spiders, cockroaches, caterpillars, and scorpions. It sits on low perches within the forest understory and waits for prey. One nest, found in June, contained a red morph female guarding a three-week-old gray morph chick. The nest was eight feet aboveground in an oak tree. It occupies montane evergreen, cloud, and moist oak-pine forests from 5,900 to 8,200 feet in elevation.

Mexico lists it as in peril of extinction, and it is globally vulnerable due to its limited distribution and ongoing habitat loss, fragmentation, and degradation. Pine-oak montane forests are logged for firewood and charcoal. Bark beetle epidemics, urbanization, agricultural, and a civil war in Chiapas, Mexico, have all accelerated deforestation within its distribution.

Total Length
6.7–7.1 inches

Wing Chord (unflattened)
5–5.7 inches

Tail 2.4–3 inches

Weight 2.2–2.5 ounces

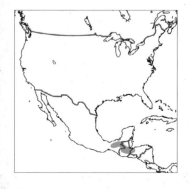

Balsas Screech Owl

Megascops seductus

The Balsas Screech Owl is a relatively large *Megascops* species sporting gray-brown plumage with a somewhat pinkish hue. It has brown to golden-brown eyes, short ear tufts, and large toes covered in bristlelike feathers. Its bill is greenish. It was first described in 1941 based on a specimen from Apatzingan, Mexico. Prior to 1998, it was a subspecies of the Western Screech Owl. Misidentification with other screech owls is not likely because its range is discrete. Its call has a rhythmic, bouncing-ball quality, with "bookh" notes that speed up to a "bobobrrr" trill. The female version of this call is higher-pitched. It also has a bold "scream" or alarm call. It is a year-round resident within a moderately small range in southwestern Mexico, and is fairly common in Jalisco, Colima, Michoacán, Morelas, and Guerrero. New surveys in areas with suitable habitat will likely reveal that the species is found elsewhere.

Like most screech owls, it is strictly nocturnal and chooses concealed perches in dense foliage or cavities to roost in by day. It hunts primarily by listening and watching for, then pouncing on, prey from perches within and along forest edges, but can also capture flying insects. While understudied, its diet is thought to be similar to other *Megascops* owls and includes insects, rodents, and other small mammals, amphibians, reptiles, and birds.

It likely nests in tree cavities made by woodpeckers in June, but no nest sites have been reported. Eggs are presumably white. Where studied, it prefers dry forests and is less common in thorn or deciduous forests, disturbed forests with secondary growth, mesquite, tall cactus, and agricultural landscapes. It lives in dry, open to partially-open habitats with scattered trees from 2,000 to 5,000 feet in elevation. The Balsas Screech Owl is classified as near threatened due to its somewhat small range, which is subject to habitat loss from agriculture, including citrus plantations and cattle ranching. There is no evidence of a population decline or significant threats, therefore its population trend is unknown.

Total Length
9.5–10.2 inches

Wing Chord (unflattened)
6.7–7.3 inches

Tail 3.5–3.9 inches

Weight 5.3–6.1 ounces

Bare-shanked Screech Owl

Megascops clarkii

This somewhat large screech owl has small ear tufts, and the lower third of its legs—as well as its toes—are bare and pinkish. Its pale yellow eyes, interrupted whitish eyebrows, and a green- to blue-gray bill are set in a cinnamon to tawny-brown facial disk. It was first described in 1935 by Leon and Estelle Kelso based on a specimen collected in Calobre, Panama. Its scientific name, *clarkii,* is a tribute to Harry Clark of Gretna, Kansas, who aided Leon as a young student.

The male's main song is a low-pitched "woogh-woogh-woogh" delivered from high perches within tree foliage and at intervals of several seconds. Another song, often uttered concurrently with the female's higher-pitched version, is a rhythmic "bubu booh-booh-booh," rising in pitch and volume for the last two notes. Aggressive fast "toot" notes are given when flying.

This nonmigratory nocturnal resident is found from northwest Columbia north through Panama and into Costa Rica. Day roosts include sites within epiphytes or dense tree vegetation. It seeks out prey at dusk and throughout the night from within tree canopies, various perches in forest openings, and along forest edges. It catches a diversity of prey off the ground or from tree branches, including invertebrates such as spiders, beetles, and grasshoppers. Small rodents and birds are also likely taken in this manner.

One nest was found in a natural cavity within the forked trunk of a large, isolated live oak tree in a pasture in Costa Rica. Young have been observed out of the nest by May to August. It inhabits thick, moist montane cloud forests and thinned woodlands, especially forest edges, in elevations ranging from 2,950 to 10,500 feet. Its response to the playback of its main song implies that it regularly maintains or defends a home range or territory.

Despite its small distribution and a lack of assessment criteria information, the IUCN has given this species a conservation status of least concern, or not at risk. It is apparently rare; logging and clearing of forests to create dairy cattle pastures within subtropical and tropical cloud forests within its range may threaten local populations.

80

Total Length

9.1–9.8 inches

Wing Chord (unflattened)

6.8–7.5 inches

Tail 3.5–4.1 inches

Weight 4.6–6.7 ounces

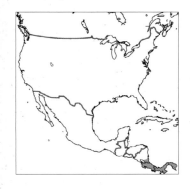

Tropical Screech Owl
Megascops choliba

This small owl with short, pointed ear tufts has variable color morphs, including cinnamon or rusty red, brown, and—most commonly—grayish-brown. Its yellow eyes, white eyebrows, blackish eyelids, and grayish-green bill are set in a gray-brown to reddish-cream mottled facial disk. It was first described in 1817 based on a specimen from Paraguay. It is also known as the Choliba Screech Owl. Its main song is a terse, purring trill denoted as "gurrrrku-kukuk," with two to three accentuated notes at the end. Females sing less frequently than males and are higher-pitched. Both sexes sing a "bububububu" song, often together, especially during courtship. Mated pairs keep in touch using a soft "wook" contact call and when alarmed they emit a hollow, laughing "hahahaha" sound.

This nonmigratory resident owl is found east of the Andes from Uruguay and Argentina, north through Central America to Costa Rica, and on the island of Trinidad. It leaves its daytime roosts in dense vegetation at dusk and is active throughout the night. The Tropical Screech Owl is able to catch bats, moths, and other insects in flight, but also catches prey on the ground, including worms, cicadas, beetles, locusts, mantids, crickets, spiders, and small vertebrates such as frogs, snakes, birds, opossums, mice, and rice rats. Breeding pairs are quite vocal during courtship, and males actively lead females to tree cavities or even artificial nest boxes. Up to three white eggs are laid, and the young grow fast, from 0.5 ounce at hatching to 3.9 ounces when twenty-four days old. They fledge at twenty-eight to twenty-nine days old.

It can live at elevations up to 9,850 feet, where montane climates are warmer and relatively drier, such as in Columbia. Elsewhere it typically lives below elevations of 4,900 feet. Throughout its range it prefers savanna or open forests, riparian forests, forests adjacent to roads, and treed parks and farmland. Its global status is least concern, as it is common in many parts of its range. Habitat loss, insecticide use, and vehicle collisions are known threats to local populations in developed areas. It is attracted to insects drawn to streetlights at night, making it prone to being killed by passing vehicles.

Total Length
7.9–9.8 inches

Wing Chord (unflattened)
6.1–7.2 inches

Tail 3.1–3.9 inches

Weight 3.5–5.6 ounces

Vermiculated Screech Owl

Megascops vermiculatus

Total Length
7.9–9.1 inches

Wing Chord (unflattened)
5.9–6.7 inches

Tail 3–3.3 inches

Weight 3.8 ounces

This medium-size screech owl has bright yellow-orange eyes; pale, inconspicuous eyebrows; and an olive-gray bill set in a rufous-brown facial disk. The facial disk has fine dark vermiculations and an indistinctly marked rim. It has short ear tufts, and its lower legs and toes are both bare and pinkish-brown. The rufous morph is like the grayish-brown color phase except that the dark feather patterns are less noticeable. The wing tips extend beyond the relatively short tail. It was first described in 1887 by Robert Ridgway based on a specimen from Costa Rica. It is often considered to be a subspecies of the Guatemalan Screech Owl, but its song is distinctly shorter. It is also known as the Little Vermiculated Duke or the Middle American Screech Owl.

Females utter a higher-pitched and shorter version of the male's main song, which is a series of "u" purring notes sung as fast as seventeen notes per second. The song starts gently, then increases in pitch and loudness, and finally drops in pitch and volume for the last few notes. A shorter version of this trill-like song is sung simultaneously by a breeding male and female. A pair also keeps in touch with a "ghoor" contact call. An aggressive "prrrowr" call with a rising inflection has been noted as well.

This nocturnal year-round resident occupies moist epiphyte-laden tropical forests from sea level up to 3,940 feet elevation from northwestern Columbia, north through Panama, and into Costa Rica. Its response to the playback of its main song is indicative of its territorial nature. There are no published longevity records or home range estimates for this species. It eats mainly insects, such as katydids and beetles, but also takes small vertebrates. It reportedly lays up to three white eggs in tree cavities. As mentioned above, it is considered by some to be a subspecies of the Guatemalan Screech Owl, which has been given a status of least concern. Therefore, the Vermiculated Screech Owl does not yet have an official global status. Local populations are likely threatened by forest habitat destruction or degradation.

Guatemalan Screech Owl

Megascops guatemalae

Total Length
7.9–9.1 inches

Wing Chord (unflattened)
6–7 inches

Tail 2.7–3.7 inches

Weight 3.2–4.3 ounces

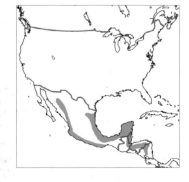

Its white-feathered eyebrows stand out near the dark, short ear tufts in both its rufous and brown forms. Yellow eyes and a greenish-yellow to gray bill are set in a light-brown to grayish or rufous facial disk that has fine vermiculations and a dark narrow or spotted border. Prior to 1998 this species was considered to be a subspecies of the Vermiculated Screech Owl until differences in its appearance, behavior, and vocalizations were discovered. It was originally described by Richard Sharpe in 1875.

The male's main song is a variable trill of "u" notes, uttered at a rate of about fourteen per second, that lasts up to twenty seconds. The female's version of this song is shorter, higher-pitched, and reportedly has a "tinny" quality. Another song is reminiscent of a table-tennis ball bouncing and is represented as "bup bup bup-bup-bupbupbupbupburrt," accelerating toward the end of the song. The female also sings a higher-pitched version of this song simultaneously with her mate as a courtship ritual.

It is nonmigratory and is found in northern Nicaragua and Costa Rica, north to Tamaulipas on the Atlantic side, and on the Pacific slope from Oaxaca to Sonora, Mexico.

It is predominantly active at night, and can be brought close enough to be seen by imitating or playing a recording of its song. Song playback must be used sparingly so as not to disturb breeding pairs. It is a secretive owl that is difficult to find by day, when it roosts in dense foliage or in tree cavities, and at night, as it typically sings from concealed perches.

The Guatemalan Screech Owl eats invertebrates such as beetles and grasshoppers, and also small fish, frogs, lizards, and mammals.

It nests between March and April, and two to five white eggs are laid in tree cavities. Its coastal range distribution reflects its preference for humid lowlands to semidry evergreen, semideciduous, and thorn forests. It is also found in dense, scrubby, and secondary-growth woodlands, from sea level to 5,000 feet elevation. Deforestation and other sources of habitat degradation or loss may pose a threat to local populations, but its current global status is least concern, or not at risk.

Puerto Rican Screech Owl

Megascops nudipes

Total Length
7.9–9 inches

Wing Chord (unflattened)
6.1–6.7 inches

Tail 3.1–3.4 inches

Weight 3.6–5.4 ounces

This small owl does not have ear tufts. It is typically gray-brown, although there is a less-common rufous color morph. The facial disk is reddish-brown with dark concentric rows and mottled, whitish eyebrows that extend to above the brownish-orange eyes and the greenish-gray bill. Its scientific name, *nudipes*, refers to its bare lower legs and bare toes. It was first described in 1800 by French biologist François Marie Daudin, based on a specimen from the Lesser Antilles. It is also known as the Puerto Rican Bare-legged Owl and the Cuckoo Bird.

"Toad-like" and "guttural" describe its quavering trill "rrurrrrr" song, which lasts up to five seconds. A shorter version sounds like "rruorr." It starts softly, gets louder and higher-pitched, then fades quickly. Female versions of these songs are higher-pitched, but when males and females duet, it often sounds as if only one owl is singing. Other sounds produced by this owl include a high-volume "coo-coo" and a muted, cackling "gu-gu," which may serve as contact calls between paired males and females.

This resident owl is endemic to Puerto Rico and a few adjacent Caribbean islands, including Isla de Culebra. It is likely extirpated from Isla de Vieques and the adjacent Virgin Islands (Tortola, St. Thomas, St. John, and St. Croix) of the Lesser Antilles due to the loss of forested habitats that has been underway since the 1600s. This nocturnal owl hides by day in rock crevices and caves, or perched in thick vegetation in shrubs and trees. It eats mainly insects, and also small vertebrates such as geckos, birds, and rodents.

It nests from April to June and lays up to four white eggs in cavities in trees, houses, or in limestone cliffs. It occupies thick forests and thickets, including those around or near human dwellings, from sea level up to 3,000 feet elevation. It has been assessed globally as not at risk, and least concern in Puerto Rico. One subspecies is extinct from Puerto Rico's offshore islands and the Virgin Islands due to deforestation. Its demise is thought to be exacerbated by egg predation by the Pearly-eyed Thrasher.

Cuban Bare-legged Owl

Gymnoglaux lawrencii

Total Length
  7.9–9.1 inches
Wing Chord (unflattened)
  5.4–6.1 inches
Tail 2.8–3.5 inches
Weight ~2.8 ounces

Whereas most owls and birds have twelve tail feathers, this one has only ten. The elongated yellow-brown legs and toes are bare, hence its common name. Its round head appears relatively small and lacks ear tufts. A yellow-gray bill, brown eyes, and white cheeks and eyebrows are set in a muted yellow to white facial disk. It is also known as the Cuban Screech Owl and Little Duke of Cuba. Molecular DNA analysis is needed to clarify its relationship to other owl species. It is the only species in the genus *Gymnoglaux,* and was first described in an 1868 London publication based on a specimen collected in Cuba.

The male's main song is a gentle "cu-cu-cu-cuencuk" or "coo-coo-coo-gu-gu-guk," which both speeds and rises in pitch toward the end. Females utter a descending but high-pitched, "yiu-yiu-yiu." It is deemed to be a common year-round resident in Cuba and on the adjacent Isla da la Juventud. The dispersal of independent juveniles and nonbreeding adults has not been documented. The Cuban Bare-legged Owl roosts by day in the obscure vegetation of trees or thickets, and also in caves, tunnels, or cracked rock. It emerges and is active at night. It is often observed on the ground in partially open areas, but can readily fly in thick-forested habitats with its short, rounded wings, using its long tail to steer. One individual reportedly lived seven years in the wild.

It hunts a variety of insects and other arthropods while on the ground, or by pouncing on its prey from a low perch. Small frogs, snakes, and birds are also eaten. These are captured in dense forests and brushy thickets, and also on plantations, and partially open limestone areas with caves and fissures. The breeding season is reported to be from January to June. Normally two white eggs are incubated by the female in nests found in holes or cracks of trees, on cliffs, or even in limestone caves. Its global status is least concern because it is reportedly common over much of the island, inferring that it has adapted well to the extensively developed habitats.

Snowy Owl
Bubo scandiacus

This large, white (or mostly white) diurnal owl has a rounded face, and it lacks feathered ear tufts. Its majestic beauty was captured in 13,000-year-old cave paintings in the Cave of the Trois-Frères in the French Pyrenees (the cave is named for three brothers who discovered it in 1914). The intense golden-yellow eyes are set in a small, incomplete facial disk. Thick, white, hairlike feathers almost obscure its black bill, toes, and talons. The feathers undoubtedly assist in keeping the owl warm during fierce winter blizzards. Juvenile and adult females are more flecked with dark spots and bars than juvenile males, which are relatively white on the neck and crown.

It was first described in 1758 by Swedish naturalist Carolus Linnaeus, and its species name refers to the Scandinavian location where it was first observed. *Nyctea scandiacus* was transferred to the genus *Bubo* in 1999 based on molecular evidence that documented its (and other owls') evolutionary history. It is the bird emblem of Quebec, Canada, where it is called the *Harfang des Neige* and *ookpik*. Other common names include the Tundra Ghost Owl and the White Terror of the North.

The male's booming territorial song is reminiscent of a hound dog's baying. It is a series of two to six rough "krooh" or "hoo" notes at one- to two-second intervals. The last note is frequently the loudest, and variations include drawn out and/or deeper notes. They sing while flying, but more frequently they sing from elevated or prominent locations within their territory, such as the crests of ridges or hills, and the sound can carry for several miles. Males are more vocal than females, especially early in the breeding season as they spend more time defending the nest site and territory from other males. Females have a higher-pitched voice and give a mew, whistlelike, or "ke-ke-ke-ke-ke" call that is associated with courtship feeding, mating, feeding young,

Total Length
   21–26 inches
Wing Chord (unflattened)
   15–18 inches
Tail 8–9.5 inches
Weight 1.6–6.5 pounds

or—more dramatically—when trying to distract predators from the nest or flightless young. Like most owls, they can snap their bill and/or hiss in response to close encounters with threatening predators like the Arctic fox. Young can snap their bill when only eight days old, and hiss when they are two weeks old. When humans approach a Snowy Owl nest, the breeding adults give a variety of threat calls denoted as strings of "rick," "kre," "ha," "how," "quork," or "quawk" notes from perches, or in flight. The notes are uttered more intensely and rapidly the closer the intruder gets to the nest. After young disperse from the nest, walking over the tundra in different directions, they give a sharp squeal that is thought to help adults returning with prey to locate their scattered young.

Some curious reports of calls in winter suggest that its vocalizations are more complex than previously thought. Owls have been heard uttering sounds like grinding teeth, screams, grunts, and quiet warbling melodies. Some of these sounds were given in flight and others were uttered while perched.

The Snowy Owl breeds, and sometimes winters, in the Arctic tundra above the tree line and on ocean shores from coastal areas up to 990 feet in elevation. Some portion of the population regularly disperses southward to winter in the northern portions of the Great Plains and

similar latitudes, both eastward and westward. Here, they occupy large open habitats such as marshes, farm fields, airports, and prairie grasslands. On rare occasions they get as far south as California, Texas, and Florida. They also live in similar areas in Eurasia.

Movements between breeding and wintering ranges have been described as nomadic in response to changes in population densities of prey on its breeding habitat. Some Snowy Owls that winter in the open habitat of Boston International Airport have been documented to return to the same prey-rich areas in successive winters.

The Snowy Owl is primarily diurnal, presumably an adaptation to nesting in Arctic sites with endless sunlight. Summer roosts and nest sites are typically atop hills or ridges, affording the owl a good view of the

surrounding tundra. Nest sites and preferred roosts are often noticeable by lush vegetation and a concentration of flowering plants nurtured by owl droppings and unconsumed parts of lemmings and other prey items. In winter, daytime hunting perches include tall utility poles or buildings. One individual was seen flying into the middle of an open field at dusk to roost overnight on the ground against a lump of frozen earth. This behavior coincided with the emergence of Great Horned Owls, a known predator of the Snowy Owls, in winter.

Snowy Owls can live to be thirty-five years old in captivity, but the oldest known wild owl lived for eleven years and seven months. While some owls, especially young ones, are known to starve to death, other owls succumb to collisions with vehicles, airplanes, or wires. Less frequently, an unknown number die from causes such as eating poisoned rodents or pigeons, being electrocuted on power lines, or from disease. In winter, young male owls are leaner than young females; adult females have the heaviest fat reserves.

Lemmings are the main prey of Snowy Owls, especially during the breeding season. When lemmings are absent, or when hunting in midcontinental wintering areas where daylight hours are limited during cold weather, this predator can nonetheless catch a surprising diversity of winter prey. Such prey includes fish, amphibians, birds, and mammals, including muskrats and jackrabbits. One pellet contained no less than twenty-seven meadow vole skulls captured in one day—a meal that weighed a conservatively estimated one to two pounds! Prey are usually captured on the ground or in the water. The speed and agility of the Snowy Owl was firmly established when one was observed chasing, then catching, a flying rock dove.

Snowy Owl nests are located on higher elevations, exposed areas such as windy hummocks, or on the Arctic tundra. From this vantage point, adults can watch for prey and predators such as Arctic foxes or wolverines approaching over great distances. The nest is a shallow depression and is lined with breast feathers from the female's brood patch. When food is plentiful, breeding pairs can raise up to a dozen young, but they may also forego nesting if prey is scarce over broad geographic areas. Incubation lasts for just over thirty days. Young owls leave the nest when about two to three weeks old, and they can fly when seven weeks old. In winter, adult females in particular defend small territories as long as prey there remains abundant, after which time they disperse in search of other locations rich with prey. Such ephemeral territories are maintained by vocalizations such as screams, with territorial defense postures, chase flights, and sometimes attacks, all directed at intruders.

The IUCN classifies the Snowy Owl as least concern, or not at risk, as it is widespread, abundant, and there are few threats to its habitat. However, there is a need to better study changes in its population and distribution, especially in light of rapid climate change in Arctic ecosystems. Wind-borne contaminants from southern industrial areas, such as persistent organic pollutants, may subject predators to sublethal effects or elevated mortality rates through a mechanism known as biomagnification—where chemicals in prey are concentrated up the food chain in top carnivores. This species has experienced a statistically insignificant decrease over the last forty years in North America. Coordinated international monitoring efforts are needed because some owls migrate between Alaska and Russia.

Great Horned Owl
Bubo virginianus

Total Length
17.7–24.8 inches

Wing Chord (unflattened)
11.7–15.4 inches

Tail 6.9–9.8 inches

Weight 2.2–5.5 pounds

This large, powerful owl has widely separated, prominent ear tufts; large yellow eyes in a medium-size facial disk; and a white bib. It has remarkably strong feet and large, thick talons. Many color phases exist, varying regionally in relation to humidity levels. Those in dry desert and subarctic habitats are pale, even whitish, while darker morphs are found in more humid coastal areas. Typical colors include black lines on a buff or brown background. Males are notably smaller than females. Its species name is derived from the Virginia colonies, which were named after the "Virgin" Queen Elizabeth I. The first specimens were collected from the colonies and described by Johann Gmelin in 1788. Historically, over twelve subspecies have been described based on this variation in coloration, and considerable debate continues on their validity.

A variable, powerful, and deep series of three to six or more notes like "who-ho-ho-ho, who-ho-ho-ho, whoo" makes up its territorial song. The notes of the male are distinctly lower-pitched than those of the female. Detailed recent studies of the vocalizations of a captive, human-imprinted female owl and wild pairs in Minnesota, revealed no less than five types of hoots, four types of chitters, and five types of squawks based on differences in the number of syllables, inflection, pitch, duration, volume, and behavior. Add hisses and bill-clacking to this and it is apparent that there is more complexity to owl auditory communication than previously thought for this—and likely all—owl species.

The Great Horned Owl is the most widely distributed of the North American owls, living from subarctic ecosystems through Central America, to the southernmost tip of the South American continent. Owls living in northern parts of its range exhibit southern or southeasterly winter irruption migrations up to 1,250 miles. Such movements occur when boreal forest or aspen parkland populations of its main prey supply (the snowshoe hare)

plummet and bitterly cold temperatures test the owl's ability to find enough food. Such dispersal movements often occur in waves, initially composed mostly of juvenile owls, followed by adult females and then adult males. However, the Great Horned Owl is more typically a permanent resident throughout its range.

In southern parts of its range, this normally nocturnal species adapts to local conditions such that it can occasionally be found hunting during the day. Daytime hunting is the norm in some areas, especially in the breeding season in northern latitudes where summer days stretch out so long that midnight seems more like dusk than night. Great Horned Owls typically hunt from a variety of perches that afford them a good view of the surrounding habitat. They will also sometimes hunt while flying over fields, or, rarely, by chasing injured prey on foot. Roost sites are as varied as the habitats in which they thrive and include trees, brush, log, or rock piles, large tree cavities, cliffs, and buildings.

The oldest known wild Great Horned Owl was an individual originally caught and banded as an adult in a forested part of Winnipeg, Canada, a city of over 650,000 people with continental climate extremes akin to Moscow, ranging from −54°F to 108°F. This tough old bird was sadly found dead on a Winnipeg road at twenty-eight years and six months old. More typical longevity records for wild Great Horned Owls range from ten to fifteen years. Life in captivity is easier, as demonstrated by one owl at the San Francisco Zoo that lived for fifty years. This female hatched in 1972 and died in April 2012.

While on average 90 percent of its prey are mammals, including small rodents, hares, and rabbits, it also feeds on a large diversity of animals ranging from aquatic beetles captured in midair to large birds such as geese and herons. Cannibalism has been observed, but it is unclear if this is the result of territorial disputes, or if it is primarily an act of predation. It is also known to eat other owl species, so smaller owls either avoid living in areas occupied by Great Horned Owls, or do so secretively. Despite the occasional owl that repeatedly returns to dine on an inadequately protected flock of chickens, farmers should generally be happy to share their land with these magnificent raptors. One Great Horned Owl can consume between five to eight rodents per day, which adds up to 2,000 to 3,000 rodents per year. Birds or mammals killed that are too large to consume in one day are guarded jealously by this species, and they feed on them for several days.

Nest sites can include stick nests built by large birds such as ravens, hawks, or herons; large tree cavities; sheltered ledges on cliffs; deserted

buildings; and artificial platforms built by humans. It nests relatively early compared to other owls, and clutch initiation appears to vary with local temperature conditions. For example, Great Horned Owls nested earlier in the warmer city microclimate of Winnipeg, compared to cooler adjacent rural areas. While this may have also been due to other factors, cities stay warmer due to the nature of concrete and buildings to absorb and radiate heat. Clutches of up to five eggs can be found in years when prey populations are high, but more typically two to three eggs are laid. Eggs hatch after about thirty days of incubation, and young may stay in the nest up to six weeks. The dispersal of young owls occurs as early as late summer.

Extreme Arctic and subalpine areas are the only habitats where this versatile owl is seemingly unable to thrive in its North, Central, and South American distribution. It is found as a year-round resident in an amazing variety of forest types, developed areas, grasslands, and deserts, making it the most extensively distributed North American owl. This owl is found from sea level to about 13,200 feet in elevation. While they do not mate for life, breeding pairs can remain together for years, even over a decade, in a breeding home range. The average home range size of the Great Horned Owl is about 640 acres, or one square mile. Home range estimates from different parts of its range vary considerably, and can cover from 366 to 2,182 acres. A study conducted in the Yukon Territory determined that home range also varied from year to year more due to owl density than changes in prey availability. Single owls, called "floaters," live furtively between such home ranges, waiting for a territory to open up, such as when a resident owl either dies or becomes too old or weak to defend its realm. Therefore it comes as no surprise that the home range size of floaters average five times that of territorial pairs.

The IUCN has assessed this owl's status as least concern, or not at risk, because it thrives in developed areas, and is widespread, abundant, and secure. The most important factor affecting populations is starvation of young owls. Predation by eagles, vehicle collisions, electrocution, and illegal hunting are other dangers. The use of strychnine or anticoagulants to poison rodent pests can result in secondary poisoning if owls consume contaminated prey. Populations of this powerful predator are sometimes reduced to protect susceptible breeding populations of endangered species such as the Peregrine Falcon or the Spotted Owl. Understandably, this action is often based on the inferred impacts of the Great Horned Owl, suggesting that more research on the actual ecological relationships between such species is needed.

Spectacled Owl
Pulsatrix perspicillata

The Spectacled Owl has fine, dark barring on its belly and adjacent areas, and a uniform sooty-black back and head. Females are larger than males. This large owl is named after the spectacled appearance created by white lores and eyebrows on a dark brown facial disk. It has yellow to blackish-brown eyes, a creamy-yellow bill, and a round head without ear tufts. The first scientific description was published in 1790 based on a specimen from Cayenne, French Guiana. It is also sometimes called the Large-collared Owl.

Both the male and female utter a song that consists of a descending and low-pitched "PUP-pup-pup-pup-po" or "PUM-PUM-pum-pum" series of notes that accelerate and then quietly trail off. The female's call is higher-pitched, and the male and female sometimes sing together in a duet. Young demand food with a whistlelike call, and females demand food with a scream-like "kerWHEEEER." It is nonmigratory and avoids being mobbed by birds by hiding in dense foliage during the day. At night it hunts within treed canopies and from the forest edges. It captures medium-size mammalian prey such as bats, agoutis, rabbits, and skunks, and also smaller rodents, insects, crabs, amphibians, reptiles, and birds, including other owl species.

The Spectacled Owl's breeding biology is different from other owls in many ways. The breeding season starts in April and continues as late as September in some parts of its range. Two eggs, sometimes three, are laid in cavities in large trees, and incubation reportedly takes five weeks, which is about a week longer than other owls. The chicks remain with their parents for up to a year. It occupies subtropical montane forests up to 4,900 feet in elevation, but also lower areas including mature dense tropical rain forests, dry forests, treed savannahs, plantations, and open areas with scattered trees. The Spectacled Owl commonly sits on branches near streams or forest edges. The IUCN lists this species as least concern because of its large range.

Total Length
 16.1–20.5 inches
Wing Chord (unflattened)
 12–14.2 inches
Tail 6.5–8.5 inches
Weight 1.3–2.2 pounds

Spotted Owl

Strix occidentalis

Total Length
    16–19 inches
Wing Chord (unflattened)
    12–13 inches
Tail 7.5–9 inches
Weight 1.1–1.7 pounds

The Spotted Owl has a yellow-green bill and a round facial disk with indistinct, brown concentric rings surrounding its dark brown eyes. It has no feathered ear tufts and is covered with the prominent, irregular white spots from which it gets its name. John Xantus de Vesey first described it in 1860. It is also known informally as the Canyon Owl and the Brown-eyed Owl.

Their alarm call is remarkably similar to a barking dog. When breeding birds are calling to locate their mates, they utter a string of scary ascending whistles that end in a sirenlike echo. Their territorial song is denoted as "who who-who whoooo" and consists of three to four drawn-out, deep-pitched hoots.

Breeding adults are typically year-round residents, but young or unpaired birds can disperse as far as 125 miles. A seasonal migration occurs in some areas, with birds moving up to forty miles from high-elevation nesting areas to lower wintering habitats with up to 4,900 foot shifts in elevation. Home range size can cover up to 18,700 acres.

The Spotted Owl is typically nocturnal. When summer temperatures exceed 80°F, it seeks out cool roost sites in order to escape temperature-related metabolic stress. Such roosts are abundant in complex multilevel

tree structures of older forests. It appears to be more tolerant of heat in the southern parts of its range, but nonetheless seeks out shady roosts among the vegetated steep walls of deep rock canyons. Roosting owls are hard to locate nestled against trees in dark, thick cover, and they are so reluctant to fly that people have been able to approach and pet them on their perches. This behavior also makes them easy to capture once they are found roosting.

While most young owls perish, adult Spotted Owls can live up to twenty-one years in the wild. In 1970 biologist Eric Forsman rescued an orphaned chick and raised it for educational and research purposes. The owl, affectionately dubbed "Fat Broad," died in February 2002, just shy of its thirty-second birthday. The owl was awarded the 2006 Lady Gray'l Award and was entered into the World Owl Hall of Fame for its lifelong contribution to Spotted Owl conservation.

It preys mainly on small to medium-size nocturnal mammals, especially dusky-footed wood rats in the southern parts of its range and, conversely, flying squirrels in the north. Like other year-round resident species that occupy fixed territories, they capture and consume a large variety of prey, ranging from insects and other invertebrates, amphibians, birds, and mammals.

Breeding female Spotted Owls lay from one to four eggs from March to May in tree cavities or on stick nests built by other birds, squirrels, or wood rats, in closed-canopy forests, but also in nests on cliff ledges in steep-walled canyons. Humid old-growth conifer and oak forests are used, especially for nesting and roosting, but the Mexican Spotted Owl also uses logged secondary pine-oak forests and rocky canyons. The extent to which they can tolerate, or even benefit, from selective logging, which may increase access to prey, is unclear. In the northern parts of its range it is found from sea level to 3,900 feet in elevation, but even higher to 8,900 feet in the southern parts of its distribution.

The expansion of the Barred Owl into the range of the Spotted Owl since the 1960s has resulted in competition for habitat, and new relationships between prey and predators, with unknown consequences. These species have hybridized at least five times. Their offspring, called Sparred Owls, are fertile. The Spotted Owl is listed as Endangered in Canada and the United States. It is near threatened globally due to its small and declining population. Its decline is speeding up due to clear-cut logging. Mexican populations are thought to be stable because forests are harvested sustainably.

Mexican Wood Owl

Strix squamulata

Total Length
11.4–13 inches

Wing Chord (unflattened)
8.7–10.4 inches

Tail 5–6.4 inches

Weight ~6.2–12.2 ounces

The Mexican Wood Owl lacks ear tufts and has a rounded head. Dark brown eyes and a pale blue-gray bill are set in a dark brown, white-rimmed facial disk with white eyebrows. It was first described in 1850 based on a specimen collected in Tehuantepec City, Mexico, where it is known as *el buho café*. Its main song is a sequence of four or more evenly spaced, loud, and froglike "kwow kwow kwow gwot" notes. The song sequence is repeated every ten or more seconds. Mated pairs utter soft hoots together in duets, and females are known to respond to the male's froglike song with a high-pitched but descending "weeooah" call.

Its South American range continues north from Ecuador and Colombia through Panama, Central America, and into Mexico. It is a year-round resident that roosts in tree cavities or in thick tree cover and is active at night. It typically hunts from low perches along the edges of forests near clearings. It is also a skilled aerial hunter that is able to catch both insects and bats in flight.

A great variety of prey are eaten, including beetles, cockroaches, grasshoppers and other larger insects, frogs, lizards, and snakes. However, nocturnal and tree-dwelling small mammals, including bats, are its main source of food.

One to two eggs are laid in February to April in existing bird nests, palm snags, or tree cavities. Incubation lasts for about twenty-eight days, and young leave the nest when only thirty or so days old. Adults guard and feed their young for another three months before the young are excluded from the breeding territory. It lives in semiarid woodlands, brush land, thorny woods, open forests, dense humid forests, coffee plantations, second-growth forests, and treed cities. It ranges from sea level up to 8,250 feet and possibly at even higher elevations.

This species is included with the Mottled Owl and classified as least concern. The Mexican Wood Owl is reportedly common in western Panama, Costa Rica, and within the Mexican lowlands portion of its range. While forest destruction is noted as a threat, it can also survive in developed areas. Vehicle collisions and pesticides likely impact some local populations.

Black and White Owl

Strix nigrolineata

Total Length
13.8–17.7 inches

Wing Chord (unflattened)
10.7–11.5 inches

Tail 6.5–7.1 inches

Weight 0.9–1.2 pounds

The Black and White Owl has white-speckled eyebrows and a yellow bill that contrasts with its dark brown eyes and black facial disk. It has a round head without ear tufts and is dark sooty-brown above, and white with fine dark brown barring below. It was described in 1859 based on a specimen from Oaxaca, Mexico. It moved from the genus *Ciccaba* to *Strix* in 1999. It is also called the Black-lined Owl. A series of three to five barking "who-who-WHOW-who" notes constitute its song by the lower-pitched male and higher-pitched female. A brief, two-note "wu-whoo" contact call is given by either sex repeatedly and helps to keep members of a pair aware of each other's presence within its home range. An agitated version of the contact call is given by the female when she defends her territory against intruding members of their species.

This generalist nocturnal predator is a year-round resident that eats insects such as dung beetles and cockroaches and fourteen different bat species. Other vertebrate prey include small nocturnal tree frogs, mice and rats, and birds. Most of its prey is captured aboveground, making this owl primarily a forest canopy hunter. It lays one to two white eggs in late March to May in depressions in arboreal orchids and epiphytes or in tree cavities. Its day roosts in dense vegetation high in the forest canopy are hard to find.

The Black and White Owl uses a variety of damp evergreen to deciduous forests, including those fragmented by ecological processes or developed areas such as villages, settlements, and plantations. It is found from sea level mangroves and woodlands near water to moist forests up to 7,870 feet. It is classified globally as least concern due to its wide distribution. Extreme and extensive forest clearing and intensive pesticide use in some areas are threats to local populations. It is regularly found in established protected areas such as Venezuela's Henry Pittier National Park.

Fulvous Owl
Strix fulvescens

Total Length
  15–19 inches

Wing Chord (unflattened)
  12–13 inches

Tail 7.3–8 inches

Weight Not available

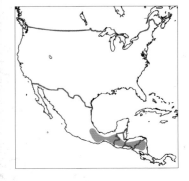

The Fulvous Owl is named for its dull reddish-yellow to brownish-yellow underparts. This large owl, also known as the Guatemala Barred Owl, lacks feathered ear tufts on its round head. Its black-brown eyes are set in an even darker brown and dark-rimmed facial disk that contrasts with its white eyebrows and bright yellow bill. The first scientific description of this species was published in 1868 based on a specimen from Guatemala. Its song is reminiscent of that of both the Barred Owl and Great Horned Owl and consists of a rhythm of short deep "who-wuhu-woot-woot" notes. The higher-pitched female will call sequentially with her mate in defense of their territory. Also heard are parrotlike nasal "gwao" single hoots. Its brazen song is frequently detected before sunrise.

The Fulvous Owl lives in a limited area of Central America that includes southern Mexico, Guatemala, Honduras, and El Salvador. It is hard to find by day in its tree cavity roosts or in dense tree foliage. This nocturnal "sit and wait" predator hunts its prey from within its territory. Nematode parasites similar to that known to infect bird eyes (the bird eyeworm *Oxyspirura*) were recovered from the cornea and nictitating membrane of a Fulvous Owl that had been captive for only three months when it died suddenly. It may have gotten the parasite from eating cockroaches, which are the parasite's intermediate host. Its diet consists of invertebrates, frogs, lizards, birds, and small mammals.

The breeding biology of this species is poorly known but it lays two to three, sometimes five, eggs in tree cavities. Young likely hatch after twenty-eight to thirty days of incubation, and have been seen out of the nest in May. It is found in montane regions from 3,900 to 9,850 feet in tropical temperate pine-oak forests and damp cloud forests. Breeding pairs defend their territory year-round, and so usually respond to playback or imitations of its song or calls. The Fulvous Owl is listed as least concern despite the fact that its global population appears to be decreasing due to ongoing habitat destruction. A conservation action plan is needed to offset the cumulative impacts of the loss of forested habitat within its restricted range.

Barred Owl

Strix varia

Total Length
16–25 inches

Wing Chord (unflattened)
12.3–15 inches

Tail 8–10 inches

Weight 1.4–2.3 pounds

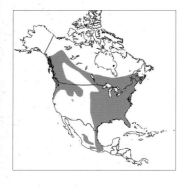

This large brownish-gray owl has no ear tufts, dark brown eyes, and a yellow bill set in a whitish-brown, dark-edged facial disk. Each eye is surrounded by four to five brownish concentric rings on a grayish-white to pale buffy gray background. It is named for the horizontal bars on its throat and upper chest and streaks on its belly. It was first described in 1799 by an amateur naturalist. It is also called the Swamp Owl and The Hooting Cat of the North. Its main call sounds like "Who cooks for you? Who cooks for you all?" A recent detailed study of its vocalizations in Florida described thirteen unique vocalizations, making this owl the vocal gymnast of the owl world. These include complex duets by breeding pairs used to defend their territories, and some sound like a frenzied monkeylike cacophony. Like most owls, female calls are higher-pitched, are more drawn-out, and have more vibrato.

The Barred Owl is found over most of the eastern half of North America from Florida to southern Canada. Over the past 140 years it expanded its range to central and western parts of the continent due to settlement of the Great Plains. This settlement resulted in the growth of trees by fire suppression, the extirpation of grazing bison and, in many locations, beaver. One unsolved question in this scenario is why it did not expand westward north of the Great Plains, through the southern

boreal forests of Manitoba and Saskatchewan before European settlement. It is a year-round resident, and pairs stay together as long as they survive. Some nest sites and territories have been used by breeding Barred Owls for decades. The dispersal of young owls is typically less than six miles before they settle and compete for a breeding home range.

It is a nocturnal bird, but it can sometimes be seen hunting in daylight in northern parts of its range in winter when prey is scarce. Daytime roosts are in dense foliage in tree canopies, against tree trunks, or in large tree cavities. It will call during daylight hours, but is mostly vocal at night. Characteristic aggressive behaviors at nest sites include physical attacks on raccoons, humans, or other perceived predators.

People have been struck in the face by territorial owls during nocturnal owl surveys after simply broadcasting Barred Owl courtship calls. A Barred Owl attack was a hypothetical alternative cause of death in one murder trial based on lacerations to the victim's scalp that were consistent with the talon configuration of a Barred Owl's foot. Other aggressive behaviors include agitated hooting, bill snapping, and wing clapping where the wings are forcibly brought together when the bird lands on perches, occasionally breaking branches.

The young of all species perish annually in great numbers, and Barred Owls lose many young to nest predation by raccoons, weasels, marten, and starvation. Despite these odds, one Barred Owl is known to have survived for twenty-four years in the wild and another up to thirty-two years in captivity.

This fast and agile predator is one of the few owl species that can fly circles around a tree while chasing, and then catching, squirrels. It eats invertebrates, fish, amphibians, reptiles (including turtles), birds, and mammals (including cats and small dogs). One person accidentally hooked a Barred Owl that had swooped down and pounced on a froglike fishing lure after he cast it into shallow water. The owl was rescued and later released.

It breeds from February to August but defends its territory year-round. Males court females by hooting and lifting their wings while swaying back and forth and stepping along a branch. Up to four white eggs are laid in tree cavities or used bird nests. Eggs hatch after thirty days of incubation, and flightless young leave the nest four weeks later. After four months, the young disperse from their parents' territory. It uses old-growth urban forests and coniferous or deciduous forests near streams, lakes, and swamps. Its territory ranges up to 6,617 acres. The Barred Owl's global status is least concern due to its large range and population, which has increased by 87 percent over four decades. The culling of Barred Owls to conserve the endangered Spotted Owl is controversial because only a little is known about how they interact.

Great Gray Owl

Strix nebulosa

Total Length
22–33 inches

Wing Chord (unflattened)
15–19 inches

Tail 11–13.6 inches

Weight 1.3–4.2 pounds

This large owl has brilliant yellow eyes and a yellow to ivory bill set in a bold facial disk that is finely barred with six or more concentric rings of brown or gray on a white base. Its relatively long legs are densely feathered, as are its feet and toes. The first specimen was described in 1772 and came from Severn, near the Hudson Bay Coast, of what is now Ontario. It has also been called the Phantom of the North, the Bearded Owl, and the Sooty Owl. In 1984 Dr. Robert Nero kept an injured nestling he called "Lady Gray'l" for education and research. This popular owl moved the species from relative obscurity to become the provincial bird of Manitoba. The Lady Gray'l Award was established by the Minnesota Owl Festival to honor its accomplishments by recognizing other captive owls following in her wing beats.

The male Great Gray Owl's song consists of a relatively low-volume series of deep "whoo" notes that speed up, then trail off while falling in pitch. A "whoooop" or a nasal "huurrrup" is uttered by the female when demanding food from her mate. Hungry young owls communicate their need for food with a "shrrriiip" akin to high-pressure steam escaping from a pipe. It breeds in Canada from western Quebec west and

northwest to British Columbia, and in the Yukon and Northwest Territories. In the United States, it breeds in northern Wisconsin and Minnesota, Alaska, Washington, Oregon, Idaho, Montana, California, and Wyoming. It also breeds in northern Eurasia. With the exception of high elevation montane populations of this species in western North America, the dispersal of this owl follows a multiyear, boom/bust cycle of its main small mammal prey. After years of abundant prey and successful reproduction, prey becomes scarce and large numbers of Great Gray Owls venture south of the northern forests into areas of dense human populations. Banding and radiotelemetry data document that these movements are less nomadic and more akin to migration as marked owls return to areas they have previously known when vole populations rebound.

This large owl is a rodent specialist, and routinely locates its small prey using sound alone when such prey are hidden from its view by vegetation, soil, or snow. It is able to catch voles up to eighteen inches below thick, ice-crusted snow. Cannibalism is very rare, as are captures of atypical larger prey including snowshoe hares and muskrats. The vast majority of its typical prey includes field voles, especially the meadow vole, and pocket gophers. It infrequently captures frogs, small birds, shrews, forest voles, mice, and squirrels.

Up to five eggs are laid in late March through April in abandoned stick nests or in the rotted tops of broken trees within forest stands. There is one record of it nesting on the ground in stunted treed muskeg in northern Manitoba. Nests are occasionally predated by bears and other carnivores attracted to the smell and noise; the female's habit of eating the feces and pellets of her young, then flying off

a distance to regurgitate them, may reduce the likelihood of predation for a few weeks. Young owls leave the nest between four and five weeks old, and can fly short distances a week or two later. The habitat requirements of the Great Gray Owl are dictated by its dependence on a limited number of prey species and its inability to make its own nest sites. It needs open habitats such as bogs, fens, or forest meadows for hunting voles or pocket gophers adjacent to mature forests for nest sites. Pairs commonly nest within 500 yards of each other in years when food supplies are abundant. Home ranges are up to 16,500 acres, and they can travel up to 500 miles between successive breeding home ranges in search of food.

Habitat loss or degradation from agriculture, peat extraction, and forestry continue to threaten some local populations. The provision of artificial nests within forested stands is an intensive activity that can mitigate site-specific nest habitat loss, but is impractical at larger landscape scales to manage regional populations. Globally it is classified as least concern, but there is a genetically distinct and endangered population of about 150 Great Gray Owls in the southern Sierra Nevada in California. The management of cattle grazing in montane meadows adjacent to breeding forest habitats known to support these endangered owls is critical to maintain healthy populations of their vole and pocket gopher prey.

123

Crested Owl

Lophostrix cristata

Total Length
  14–17 inches

Wing Chord (unflattened)
  11–12.8 inches

Tail 6.7–8.5 inches

Weight 0.9–1.4 pounds

This unusual-looking medium-size owl has long, protruding, whitish ear tufts that appear to extend from its white eyebrow markings to form a striking white "V" pattern pointing to its yellowish to dark gray bill. There are two distinct color morphs. One is an overall dark brown with paler underparts. It has orange-yellow eyes that are set in a rufous, black-rimmed facial disk. The paler morph has a tawny to chestnut facial disk with dark brown eyes, and is a plain gray-brown to buff color above, with whitish under parts. It is the only species in the genus *Lophostrix*. The first scientific description was published in 1800 based on a specimen from Guiana. The Crested Duke and the White Horned Owl are two of its informal common names. Its typical call is a low-pitched and repetitive "k-k-kk-kk-kkkrrrrrroa" that is also described as a rolling, deep growl, or a frog-like croak. It is regularly repeated every five to ten seconds. A short call has also been depicted as "gurrr" or "g-g-g-ggrrrr."

It is widespread from Mexico south to northern Bolivia and central Brazil, including parts of the Amazon basin. It is found in Belize, Bolivia, Brazil, Colombia, Costa Rica, Ecuador, El Salvador, French Guiana, Guatemala, Guyana, Honduras, Mexico, Nicaragua, Panama, Peru, Suriname, and Venezuela. A nocturnal owl, it is often first detected by its distinct song and calls. During the day it roosts close to the ground in dense vegetation. Large caterpillars, grasshoppers, beetles, and other insects are common prey items. It undoubtedly also eats small birds and mammals, and other vertebrate prey.

One nest was reported in the loft of a house, but it usually nests in natural tree cavities from February to May, with young owls remaining with adults into September. It is found in woodland corridors along rivers or wetlands and in moist, thick subtropical, tropical, and montane forests from sea level to 6,400 feet. The IUCN classifies the Crested Owl as least concern. The conservation of local habitat can be supported by ecotourism that offers sustainable economic benefits to local communities as alternatives to intense deforestation.

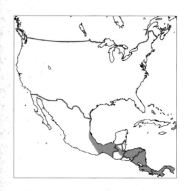

Northern Hawk Owl

Surnia ulula

This medium-size owl gets its name from its resemblance to hawks. Its wide, round head is devoid of ear tufts. The yellow, black-edged bill and yellow eyes are framed by a small, black-rimmed, whitish facial disk. It was first described by Carolis Linnaeus in 1758. Other informal common names include the Hudsonian Hawk Owl and Canadian Owl. The call of the breeding male can be imitated by blowing slowly into a cork-ball type referee's whistle. Its song consists of a fast, three- to four-second-long musical, rolling trill denoted as "kuhurrrrrrrrrrrrrr."
A fast, high-pitched chitter is given by some Hawk Owls when they are captured, held, and banded, whereas others remain quiet. Curiously, this chitter is also uttered by both members of a breeding pair when excited and close to each other. A harsh alarm "yip" or "shhhrrryip" call is repeated for long periods when the nest or young are disturbed. A softer version of the latter call is used by young owls out of the nest when hungry, or in the presence of an adult returning with prey.

The Northern Hawk Owl breeds and winters throughout its boreal forest range, but every three to five years, after experiencing local to regional abundant food supplies and successful reproduction, hundreds venture southward in what is called a winter owl invasion. This presumption is based on the high proportion of young that are captured, banded, and released, and among specimens found dead, in southern areas.

Total Length
  14–16 inches
Wing Chord (unflattened)
  8.6–10.2 inches
Tail 6.3–8 inches
Weight 7.6–13.8 ounces

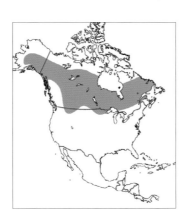

The invasion may occur periodically due to multiyear or cyclic decreases in food availability (e.g., prey crashes) on their northern home ranges, or the owls may simply be escaping more energetically challenging cold winters. As spring advances, all or most of the surviving owls are thought to return to their more northern breeding grounds. One banded hawk owl traveled 1,969 miles from Alberta, Canada, north to Alaska.

Its fearless nature and diurnal habits permit bird watchers, researchers, and local residents to observe it closely for hours, much to their delight. Many bird watchers travel great distances to see this charismatic owl in winter at the southern edges of the boreal forest. It roosts within forested stands at night, and has been observed flying for such cover from open areas when Great Horned Owls emerge at dusk to start hunting. The Northern Hawk Owl detects its prey mainly by eyesight while perching on high treetops or telephone poles in open areas with a commanding view of the surroundings. We have seen them spot, and then fly to and catch, a mouse running across a snow-covered field from as far as half a mile away. This owl lacks the dramatic ear asymmetry found in owls that routinely detect prey by sound alone. Nonetheless, it can hover over a field and locate, dive-plunge into snow or grass, and capture concealed rodents under cover up to a foot thick, presumably using only sound to locate its unsuspecting prey. Most studies describe its summer diet as primarily small rodents such as squirrels, mice, lemmings, and voles. It also eats juvenile snowshoe hares, grouse, ptarmigans, and even waterfowl. It is a formidable avian predator, which is why it has been the only owl trained by falconers to hunt birds.

It occupies muskeg, burned-over areas, open coniferous or coniferous-deciduous areas of boreal forests and aspen parkland. In montane regions it has been found up to 6,000 feet in elevation. It lays up to nine white eggs from March to June in the rotted-out hollows atop broken-off tree snags, or in old pileated woodpecker or enlarged flicker nest tree cavities. In exceptional years, when prey is plentiful, up to thirteen egg clutches have been reported. Young hatch after twenty-five to thirty days incubation, and they usually leave the nest twenty-one days later. Adults feed their young for up to three months, and young can breed the following spring. One winter home range for a male in Manitoba, was 124 acres, whereas in Norway its combined breeding and winter home range was anywhere from 350 to 2,000 acres. Its global status is least concern due to its extremely large range and population. Basic information on its natural history is anecdotal and restricted to a few accessible study areas within the boreal forest. More research is needed on its home range, habitat use, diet (especially in winter), breeding dispersal, and the behavioral context of its vocalizations.

Northern Pygmy Owl

Glaucidium californicum

The plumage on the back of the Northern Pygmy Owl's head looks like a face complete with false black eyes and a black nose or beak. Predators approaching the owl from behind may be reluctant to attack if they are fooled into thinking that the owl is looking at them. In this manner, the owl has a reduced chance of being ambushed while hunting or roosting. One study even documented that mobbing birds actually avoided the false eyespots more than the owl's real eyes. Its actual face has yellow eyes and a yellowish-white or gray bill, and no ear tufts. There are no differences in appearance between males and females. It is brownish-gray with whitish-brown spots on the forehead, sides, and back, and has dramatic dark brown streaks on a white chest. Their white-barred tail is narrow and long.

It was first described in 1857 based on a specimen from Calaveras, California, from where it obtained its scientific species name. There are many color variations of this species within its range that make the description and separation of subspecies challenging. Nonetheless, at least three subspecies are recognized. It is visually distinct from other owls in its range, and only overlaps slightly with the similar-looking, but distinct-sounding, Ferruginous Pygmy Owl in southern Arizona. In this area, the latter is typically found at lower elevations. Further research is needed on Pygmy Owl vocalizations, genetics, and ecology to untangle the controversial and unresolved classification of this group of interesting owls. Other informally used common names include the Dwarf Owl and the Rocky Mountain Owlet.

The main and commonly heard call of the Northern Pygmy Owl is a sequence of regularly spaced "toot" notes. It also utters a trill that is frequently succeeded by a "toot" or two.

Its distribution includes southeastern Alaska, British Columbia, southwestern Alberta, and parts of Washington, Oregon, Idaho, Montana, Wyoming, Utah, Colorado, Arizona, New Mexico, Nevada, California, and

Total Length
6.7–7.5 inches

Wing Chord (unflattened)
3.4–4.1 inches

Tail 2.4–3.1 inches

Weight 2.2–2.6 ounces

Mexico. Evidence is mounting about its distribution expanding eastward in Canada and parts of the United States. It is unclear the extent to which this species is nomadic, migratory, or a year-round resident, and perhaps its dispersal behavior is regularly diverse or adaptable. In montane regions it is thought to undergo an altitudinal migration upslope in spring and summer, and downslope in winter. In some areas you can hear its "toot" song year-round, suggesting that it may be a permanent resident.

It is an easy owl to locate and observe close up due to its bold nature and diurnal hunting habits. It often detects prey by sight, is mainly active at dusk and dawn, and is rarely heard or seen at night. Its presence is often made known by mobs of songbirds giving loud alarm calls directed at it or chasing it. It is also often seen hunting birds and small mammals attracted to bird feeders.

There is no information on the longevity of this species, but the similar-size Eurasian Pygmy Owl has lived up to six years in the wild and up to seven years in captivity.

It has a diverse diet that includes invertebrates such as moths and beetles, lizards, snakes, birds, and mammals. Females tend to capture relatively more mammals, some as large as red squirrels, whereas males take more birds, often as big as thrushes and jays. Clearly this small owl is both a bold and fierce predator, as it can subdue prey twice its size.

The Northern Pygmy Owl is an obligate cavity nester, and nest sites built by woodpeckers are sometimes clustered in one or a few snag trees in suitable hunting habitats. This sometimes results in a number of nest cavity-dependent species sharing the same nest tree when prey populations are high. This owl has thus been recorded as nesting concurrently in the same tree, or adjacent to, Northern Saw-whet Owls and Pileated Woodpeckers. Up to seven white eggs are laid in late March to June. Incubation lasts about twenty-eight days, and young leave the nest when twenty-three days old. In California, it prefers older forests consisting of pine, cedar, fir, and oak, including second-growth and fragmented remnants. Elsewhere it occupies the edges of coniferous and deciduous forests adjacent to meadows and lakes, and from deciduous bottom lands and foothill oak savannahs to montane forests up to 7,200 feet. In Washington the breeding home range size estimates for three males ranged from 4,200 to 5,700 acres.

The IUCN classifies the Northern Pygmy Owl as least concern because it has a very large distribution, an estimated population of over 10,000 individuals, and an increasing population based on volunteer-based surveys over the last forty years. It appears to have few, if any, threats, and it is unknown why extensive areas of otherwise suitable habitats remain uninhabited. While there are some excellent detailed studies on its biology from California, Montana, and Washington, it remains poorly studied across its vast distribution in western North America.

Below: The face-like pattern on the back of the Northern Pygmy Owl's head reduces its chances of being ambushed. Predators are reluctant to attack if they think that the owl is looking at them.

133

Cape Pygmy Owl

Glaucidium hoskinsii

Total Length
  5.9–6.7 inches
Wing Chord (unflattened)
  3.4–3.5 inches
Tail 2.4–2.6 inches
Weight 1.8–2.3 ounces

The Cape Pygmy Owl has a yellow-gray bill, yellow eyes, and thin, white eyebrows set in a brownish facial disk with no feathered ear tufts. The back of the head and neck have two lighter-edged dark triangle areas that slightly resemble eyespots. Males are less reddish than females. A 2006 DNA study demonstrated that it is evolutionarily distinct from the Northern and Mountain Pygmy Owls, which is corroborated by its distinct vocalizations. The Cape Pygmy Owl was originally described by William Brewster in 1888 from a specimen in its restricted range in Baja California. It was given its scientific name in honor of Francis Hoskins, a bird collector in the nineteeth century. It is sometimes called the Baja Pygmy Owl.

The most commonly heard call of the Cape Pygmy Owl is its distinct territorial song, which is comprised of a slow series of up to five "hoo" hoots followed by regularly spaced single or double "hoo" or "whew" notes, with five to fifteen seconds between sets.

The Cape Pygmy Owl has a restricted and isolated high-elevation mountain distribution, including the Sierra de la Giganta, Sierra Victoria, and the Sierra de la Laguna Mountains at the tip of Baja California. It is mainly a year-round resident, but many likely migrate to lower elevations in winter and infrequently to northern Baja California. It is not often heard or observed at night, leading people to conclude that it is only active during the day, including dawn and dusk.

It eats invertebrates and small birds, and, less frequently, small mammals. It lays its eggs in tree cavities and occupies pine and pine-oak forests from 4,900 to 6,900 feet in elevation, but in winter it also inhabits deciduous oak woodland forests at elevations as low as 1,640 feet. It is rare to fairly common, and is threatened due to its restricted range and habitat loss or degradation. It is not currently recognized as a full species by the IUCN and therefore has not yet been assessed globally. Parts of its range have received international recognition as significant conservation areas, such as the Sierra de la Laguna.

Mountain Pygmy Owl
Glaucidium gnoma

Total Length
5.9–6.7 inches

Wing Chord (unflattened)
3.4–3.5 inches

Tail 2.4–2.6 inches

Weight 1.8–2.3 ounces

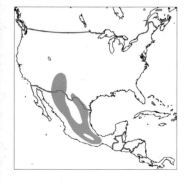

This small, dark to reddish-brown owl has pointed wings, a shorter tail, and a different song than the similar-looking but larger Northern Pygmy Owl. It has no ear tufts and its yellow eyes are accented by whitish eyebrows within its facial disk. Males are similar in appearance to females. It was first described in 1832 from a specimen from Mexico, but its status as a full species has varied considerably over time. Some experts consider it to be one of many subspecies of the Northern Pygmy Owl, along with the Cape and Guatemalan Pygmy Owls. However, its distinct song and recent DNA evidence have convinced others to treat it as a full species.

It replies to the playback of recordings of its main territorial song, which is a string of short single or double staccato "gew" notes uttered more rapidly than the single-note call of the Northern Pygmy Owl. This tiny year-round resident is distributed from Oaxaca in south-central Mexico to southwestern New Mexico and southern Arizona.

It is commonly found at dusk or dawn, and sometimes during the day, hunting within or along the edges of forests. Various invertebrates are consumed, including grasshoppers, beetles, and crickets, and also vertebrates such as amphibians, small lizards and other reptiles, small to medium birds, and small mammals.

The breeding season extends from April to August, and as many as four white eggs are laid in tree cavities such as old woodpecker nest holes. It reportedly is found at elevations from 4,900 to 11,500 feet in mountainous pine, mixed pine-oak or oak forests, and other moist evergreen woods. In northern parts of its range it is most often found on south-facing forested slopes. Some sources have reported it to live at elevations above 4,500 feet. It is not currently recognized as a full species by the IUCN, and therefore it does not have a global status assessment. In 1998 it was lumped with (and called) the Northern Pygmy Owl.

Guatemalan Pygmy Owl

Glaucidium cobanense

Total Length
6.3–7.1 inches

Wing Chord (unflattened)
3.2–3.9 inches

Tail 2.6 inches

Weight No data available

The Guatemalan Pygmy Owl is small and has two color forms: brown, or more commonly, very reddish-brown. It has yellow eyes and feet, a yellowish-ivory bill, white eyebrows and chin, and either a pale reddish-buff or brownish facial disk, with thin, reddish streaks emanating outward from its eyes. It has no ear tufts. A pair of brownish-white-edged blackish eyespots characteristic of many pygmy owls are present on the back of its head. The less common brownish form is similar, but has whiter, more pale markings. It was formerly a subspecies of the Mountain Pygmy Owl and was first described by Richard Sharpe in 1875 from a specimen collected in Coban, Guatemala.

The male's main song is a drawn-out sequence of up to 300 single or double whistlelike "toot" or "pupuhp" notes, where the latter paired note is higher-pitched and sounds like "pupuhp-pupuhp-pupuhp-pupuhp-pupuhp-pupuhp." A recent study of this species in the highlands of Guatemala, Chiapas, Mexico, described four adult vocalizations and concluded that its territorial "toot" calls are distinctly faster (3.4 notes per second) than from those of the Mountain Pygmy Owl (two notes per second). During copulation the female uttered a fast (thirty-six notes per second) series of two to three chirping notes resembling "krikrikri," while the male gave the aforementioned soft "toot" note series.

It is a year-round resident in the highlands of northern Central America southeast of the isthmus of Tehuantepec, and is restricted to Honduras, Guatemala, and southeastern Mexico. It is active during daylight, especially at dawn and dusk. There are no longevity records for the Guatemalan Pygmy Owl. It eats invertebrates, small birds, and mammals such as rodents. It lays up to four white eggs in tree cavities in highland forest habitats and volcanic highlands above 4,920 feet. Its global conservation status is unknown, but threats include habitat destruction. Some of its habitat within the north-central American highlands is recognized as an endemic bird area.

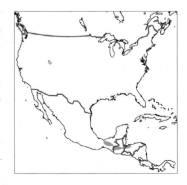

Costa Rican Pygmy Owl

Glaucidium costaricanum

Total Length
  5.7–6.7 inches
Wing Chord (unflattened)
  3.5–3.9 inches
Tail 2–2.3 inches
Weight 1.9–3.5 ounces

The brown color morph of this small owl is more common than that of its rufous form. It does not have feathered ear tufts, but there are black false eyespots, edged with white to buff, on the back of its head and upper neck. Its yellow eyes, yellow-gray bill, and white eyebrows are set in a brown-rufous mottled facial disk with streaks emanating from the area around its eyes to the outer edge of the disk. It was first described in 1937 based on a specimen from Costa Rica. Recently documented differences in its main song have convinced biologists that it is not a subspecies of the Andean Pygmy Owl. The male's main song is a long series of single-, double-, or triple-clustered tooting "dew" notes, which can be heard in the late afternoon, throughout the night, or in the early morning. Its taxonomic relationship to the Mountain, Cloud Forest, and Guatemalan Pygmy Owls needs to be examined in more detail.

The distribution of the Costa Rican Pygmy Owl is the mountainous areas of western (and perhaps eastern) Panama and in Costa Rica, and needs further study. It is nonmigratory. It is active at night, but is also regularly seen by day. It roosts in forest canopies. A variety of prey are taken by quick, short attacks from concealed perches. Insects figure prominently in its diet, but other small animals such lizards, birds, and mammals are also eaten.

Starting in March, up to three white eggs are laid in a tree cavity. The canopy and edges of cloud and montane forests are the preferred haunts of this feisty owl, but it is also found in high-altitude pastures and plains, perched within scattered groups of trees. It is typically found from about 3,000 feet in elevation up to the montane forest timberline. When agitated, it (and other Pygmy Owls) jerks its tail sideways.

Habitat destruction and pesticides are threats to this range-restricted species. It is rare in Panama, but common in the mountains of Costa Rica, such as in the Cerro de la Muerta. Its population size and trend are unknown, but it is classified as least concern by the IUCN.

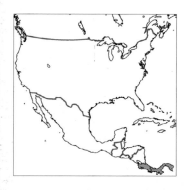

Cuban Pygmy Owl

Glaucidium siju

Total Length
  6.7 inches
Wing Chord (unflattened)
  3.4–4.3 inches
Tail 2.1–2.9 inches
Weight 1.9–3.3 ounces

This small owl lacks ear tufts on its rounded head. Most are brownish-gray, but some are an overall reddish color. The yellow eyes and narrow, whitish eyebrows are set in a dusky-specked, gray-brown facial disk. The top of the head has white spots, and the back of the head has false eyespots. One curious difference between this owl and other Pygmy Owls is that the grayish-yellow fleshy part around the base of its brownish-yellow bill does not appear swollen. It was first described in 1839 by Alcide Dessalines Orbigny.

Both males and females utter a fast string of twittering notes depicted as "wewewhititititirrr" that speed up and increase in pitch. The male's main song is a series of whistled "jiu" hoots that are emitted at regular four-second intervals. It is a nonmigratory, year-round resident owl endemic to the islands of Cuba and the Isla de la Juventud. Like other Pygmy Owls, it is partly diurnal. This results in it being mobbed by small birds as it patrols its territory. More research is needed on its longevity and other aspects of its biology, but it likely lives as long as other Pygmy Owls. Insects and small reptiles make up most of its diet. It catches these, and occasionally small birds and mammals, from perches.

During the dry season, females use tree and other cavities for nesting. Old woodpecker holes are often chosen for nest spots. Up to four white eggs are incubated by the female. Further studies are needed to verify that its breeding biology is similar to that of other Pygmy Owl species. The Cuban Pygmy Owl lives in a variety of coastal and montane forests up to 4,920 feet. It also uses partially open woods, plantations, parks with older trees, and shrubby or second-growth habitats. The Cuban Pygmy Owl has been assessed as not at risk, or least concern, by the IUCN due to its estimated global population size of more than 10,000 owls and inferred population stability. While it appears to be locally common, and it seems to use a variety of natural and developed habitats, it would benefit from a systematic population survey.

Tamaulipas Pygmy Owl

Glaucidium sanchezi

Total Length
  4.7–6.3 inches
Wing Chord (unflattened)
  3.4–3.7 inches
Tail 2–2.2 inches
Weight 1.8–1.9 ounces

The Tamaulipas Pygmy Owl is distinct from other Pygmy Owls in that the male and female are colored differently. The front of the head of either sex lacks ear tufts and is delicately marked with white to pale brown spots. Males are brown-gray on the top of the head and on the back of the neck, and are gray-olive-brown on the back, whereas the upper parts of females are tinged with cinnamon and appear reddish. As with most owls, the males are smaller than the females. The Tamaulipas Pygmy Owl was originally described from five specimens in 1949, and its species name comes from Carlos Sanchez Mejorada Jr. of Mexico in honor of his dedication to the advancement of the study of Mexican birds. In 1998 it was officially split off from the Least Pygmy Owl.

The principal call of this species is a hollow and high-pitched sequence of two or three "phew" notes, which is sometimes preceded by a wavering whistle. Its distribution is restricted to southern Tamaulipas and eastern San Luis Potosí in the mountains of northeastern Mexico. Its range may be extended farther south with additional field inventories. It lives at higher elevations and in more closed humid forests than the larger, more open habitat–based Ferruginous Pygmy Owl where their ranges overlap.

It hunts at dawn and dusk, and also occasionally during the day; however, its natural history is poorly known. There is limited information on its diet, but it's known to eat insects and small reptiles. It lays between two to four white eggs in tree cavities. The young are able to fly short distances when they leave the nest. It lives in moist evergreen cloud and other semideciduous forests between 2,950 and 6,900 feet in elevation. The status of this bird is unknown, although it is thought to be common in its restricted range. Logging may threaten some local populations. The IUCN lists it as least concern, or not at risk, based on an inferred stable but moderate population that is estimated to be greater than 20,000 individuals.

Colima Pygmy Owl

Glaucidium palmarum

Total Length
 5.1–5.9 inches

Wing Chord (unflattened)
 3.2–3.5 inches

Tail 2–2.2 inches

Weight 1.5–1.7 ounces

The Colima Pygmy Owl is similar in size to the world's smallest owl, the Elf Owl. Its eyes are yellow and its head lacks ear tufts. The back of the head has false eyespots set above a narrow cinnamon band, and the crown and nape (back of the neck) are densely covered with white to pale brown spots. The feet are bright yellow-orange, and males and females are similar in appearance. While it was originally described in 1901, it was recognized as a separate species from the Least Pygmy Owl in 1997. It is distinguished from the similar-looking Mountain Pygmy Owl by its smaller size and distinct voice.

The primary song of the Colima Pygmy Owl is a commonly heard string of twenty or more evenly spaced, hollow, hooting "whew" notes. There is usually a gap of ten or more seconds between sets of calls. Another unique alarm or territorial dispute call is given when the owl is in flight, typically late in the day. It is found from central Sonora south to Oaxaca in western Mexico. It is nonmigratory, usually active at dusk and dawn, and is rarely heard or seen at night. Even though it is a small owl, it is a fierce bird of prey that captures and kills birds and other animals twice its size. It also eats insects and reptiles.

In May it lays from two to four eggs in old woodpecker nest cavities or other holes in trees. The first specimen was collected from a palm forest in 1897. It is also found in many other habitat types, including partly deciduous pine-oak forests, coffee plantations, thorn, and drier tropical woodlands. Sometimes it is found in swamps or ravines and from sea level to 5,000 feet. The IUCN lists it as least concern, or not at risk, because it has a large range and a stable population, estimated to be moderate at more than 20,000 individuals. It is thought to be common within its range and to have no significant threats. Like many owls, its global status is actually unknown or inferred due to the absence of data.

Central American Pygmy Owl

Glaucidium griseiceps

Total Length
  5.1–7.1 inches

Wing Chord (unflattened)
  3.3–3.5 inches

Tail 1.8–2 inches

Weight 1.8–2 ounces

The Central American Pygmy Owl has yellow eyes; short, white eyebrows; and a yellow-greenish bill set in a light, brownish-gray facial disk that is flecked with white. It lacks ear tufts, and the upper and central breast has a white area that extends to the throat. The lower parts are streaked reddish-brown on white, and the upper parts are deep brown to gray-brown on the top of the head and back of the neck, and marked with small white spots. Its short, dark brown tail has two to three incomplete bars. Its unique plumage colors and patterns readily separate it from other pygmy owls. It was first described in 1875 from a specimen from the Alta Vera Paz tropical lowlands of Guatemala, and was formerly considered a subspecies of the geographically disjunct, and vocally distinct, Least Pygmy Owl until 1998.

The male's advertisement and territorial song is an interesting rapid sequence of ringing and hollow-sounding "pew" notes that start with two to four eclectic pews, and then a steady five-second-long series of about eighteen notes, uttered at three per second. More detailed studies on this song, its wavering trills, and other possible sounds are needed. Song sequences are repeated at inconsistent intervals. It is a year-round resident from Panama north through Central America and into southeastern Mexico.

It is partly active during daylight, but also energetic at night. Roosting and hunting perches are located within forest canopies and along forest edges, from which it scans for prey, attacking with a fast swoop and pounce. This Pygmy Owl eats invertebrates such as large insects and spiders, lizards, and small mammals, but its main diet is small birds such as tanagers and honeycreepers. It lays up to four white eggs in April or May in tree or termite mound cavities. It is found from sea level to 4,265 feet in mature cocoa plantations, open forests, secondary growth, and humid tropical, brushy, and evergreen forests. The bigger Ferruginous Pygmy Owl likes more open habitats. It is locally common, but logging has reduced some populations. Its global status is least concern.

Ridgway's Pygmy Owl

Glaucidium ridgwayi

The Ridgway's Pygmy Owl has a gray-brown and a rufous color morph. It has lemon-yellow eyes, white eyebrows, and a grayish-yellow or greenish-yellow bill set within a white-flecked facial disk, above a whitish throat patch. Early specimens included one collected in 1872 near Tucson, Arizona, and another in 1873 from Mexico, near Central America. Not all biologists recognize this as a full species; rather, they consider it to be a subspecies of the Ferruginous Pygmy Owl. The male's song is a rapid sequence of ten to sixty "poip" or "whoip" bell-like notes. Other sounds produced include a series of "chuck" notes, "khiu" notes, high-pitched yelping and twittering following a fast "whi-whi-whi" call, and single notes.

Total Length
6.7–7.5 inches

Wing Chord (unflattened)
3.2–4.5 inches

Tail 2.1–3.1 inches

Weight 1.6–3.6 ounces

It is a year-round resident from the northwestern tip of South America and into Panama, north to Sonora and Tamaulipas, Mexico, and into the southwestern United States. It is most active at dawn and dusk, but can also be found hunting during daylight and singing at night. It ambushes prey from concealed perches in bushy shrubs. They are occasionally spotted sitting atop exposed perches such as large cacti. Its diet is comprised mainly of invertebrates, including large insects like crickets and grasshoppers. It also eats small vertebrates such as amphibians, skinks and other lizards, birds, and mammals, some of which are larger than this tiny predator.

Up to five white eggs are laid in March in cavities in sandbanks, trees, large cacti, and termite mounds. Incubation lasts thirty days and owlets fledge when twenty-seven days old, then disperse after seven weeks. It has been found in a variety of habitats up to 6,230 feet in elevation, including both pristine and secondary-growth forests, plantations, suburban gardens and parks, palm thickets, mesquite, saguaro cacti, brush and thorny scrub, riparian forests in foothills, and tropical lowlands. The IUCN does not recognize this species as distinct from the Ferruginous Pygmy Owl (least concern), therefore there is no global assessment of its status. However, it is listed as endangered in Arizona and Texas.

Elf Owl

Microthene whitneyi

The diminutive Elf Owl is the world's smallest owl, although a few other species in South America are almost as small. It has lemon-yellow eyes, white eyebrows, and a greenish-yellow to olive-colored bill set in a cinnamon-brown facial disk, with white spots along the bottom edges. The combination of its desert home, tiny size, and nocturnal habits make it easy to identify. It was first described in 1861, and its scientific species name is derived from the famed American geologist Josiah Dwight Whitney. Other common names include Whitney's Elf Owl and Dwarf Owl.

During the breeding season, it can be located by its distinct song, a series of five to twenty high-pitched "yips." Breeding pairs will sing together with the male starting and the female chiming in a few quiet, shorter notes. Most calls are uttered by both sexes, including a downward "kweeo, kweeo" repeated at various intervals, and a stretched, sad-sounding "hee-ew" that is hard to locate. Songs and calls are heard starting at dusk, and continue in the early evening and throughout the night. A rough or raspy call is given repeatedly by the young when hungry.

It is found in arid areas of the southwestern United States to central Mexico and Baja California, and it is completely migratory in the northern parts of its range (e.g., in the United States), but a year-round resident elsewhere. The

Total Length
  4.7–5.5 inches
Wing Chord (unflattened)
  3.9–4.5 inches
Tail 1.8–2.1 inches
Weight 1.3–1.9 ounces

degree to which migratory and nonmigratory individuals mix or interact in the southern parts of its range is unknown.

The Elf Owl is nocturnal, perhaps by necessity, because when you are such a small owl it seems that every predator is out to get you, including snakes, other owl species, and ringtail and feral domestic cats. However, Elf Owls are somewhat protected by living in habitats that support a few owl and other predatory species, and by nesting in small cavities. A resourceful hunter, it pounces on prey from low perches and sometimes hangs from plants waiting for insects drawn to the fragrant or flamboyant flowers. They are adept at catching flying insects in flight, but undoubtedly the most interesting hunting behavior to observe is when it sprints after prey on foot. This tiny owl prefers to hide or flee under most circumstances, and its flight is slightly erratic, or batlike. When perched, they are upright and their legs almost touch half-way up, giving them a knock-kneed appearance. Insects and other invertebrates, such as scorpions, locusts, mantids, grasshoppers, fly larvae, caterpillars, centipedes, and cicadas, form the bulk of the Elf Owl's diet, but sometimes it will also eat small snakes, lizards, and young rodents. It

removes large indigestible or
dangerous parts from its prey
before eating them, such as the
wings of big moths or the
poisonous stingers of scorpions.

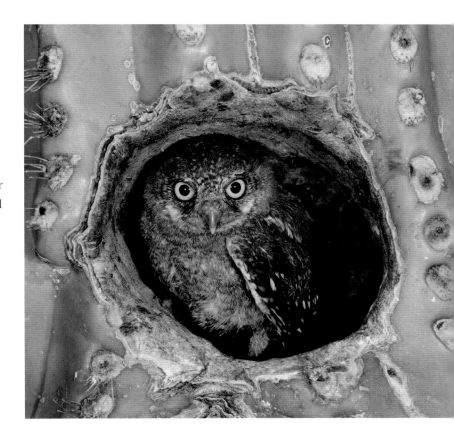

The Elf Owl is known to
cooperatively defend its nest—
and those of other birds—from
predators, as up to sixteen other
kinds of cavity-nesting birds will
use the same nest tree, or one
in the immediate vicinity.
Courtship calling increases from
April to June, and females
sometimes occupy their chosen
nest cavities to prevent other
bird species from using them
before they lay up to five eggs
in April or May. Nests are from
ten to thirty-three feet high—
often old woodpecker nest
cavities—in cacti, trees, yucca
flower stalks, utility poles, fence posts, and bird nest boxes. Males will
sometimes take short turns incubating the eggs while the female forages,
and incubation reportedly takes only two weeks. Young are fed as often
as once per minute, and fledge when four to five weeks old. It is
commonly associated with dry or desert habitats, especially those with
saguaro cacti, but is more common in subtropical thorn scrub, mesquite,
montane evergreen, and riparian woodlands up to about 7,200 feet. It
has also adapted to developed habitats. Breeding-season territories are
small, with adults ranging only up to 230 feet from their nest sites. As
many as eleven pairs nest per square mile.

Its global status is least concern based on its large range and
population. One subspecies (*M. w. graysoni*) restricted to Socorro in
Mexico's Revillagigedo Islands is probably extinct as it has not been
found since 1931. It is endangered in California, but is abundant in
Arizona and Sonora, Mexico. It may continue to expand its range in
western Texas and beyond if global warming creates new desert habitat.

Burrowing Owl

Athene cunicularia

This small brown owl is smaller than a pigeon but larger than a robin. It is easy to observe as it is active by day and is bold, allowing people to get close. As owls go, it has relatively long, sparsely feathered legs, bristled toes, and a short tail. These features are suitable for running over the prairie, and in and out of its underground nesting or roosting burrows—typically built by fossorial mammals. Its flat-topped or rectangular small head lacks ear tufts, and its yellow eyes, white eyebrow markings, and light gray to yellowish bill are set in a smallish facial disk, underscored by a bold white stripe on its chin. The Burrowing Owl was originally described in 1782 in Chile. Other common names that it has been called include the Ground, Tunnel, Prairie Dog, Rattlesnake, Cuckoo, and Gopher Owl; and in older literature it may appear within the genus *Speotyto*.

This charismatic owl utters many calls, including rasps, chatters, whistles, shrieks, and a laughing "cuhooh" or "who-who." The latter is the male's main call, usually sung near the burrow, to attract a mate or to defend his territory. When adults perceive a threat they utter a terse, low "chuck" or "epp" call to warn other owls. If a predator enters a burrow, or if young Burrowing Owls feel threatened, they can imitate the buzzy sound made by rattlesnakes.

Burrowing Owls are found in most prairie or grassland habitats in the

Total Length
7.1–11 inches

Wing Chord (unflattened)
5.6–7.9 inches

Tail 2.5–4.5 inches

Weight 5.2–8.5 ounces

Americas, including Canada west of Ontario, the United States west of the Mississippi Valley, and the drier areas of south and central Florida; the Caribbean Islands; and Mexico south to Argentina, Paraguay, and Uruguay, but they are not found within forested areas of Central America and the Amazon basin. It has not been seen since the late 1800s on the islands of Guadeloupe, Antigua, and Barbuda. Populations in southern California, south of Mexico, and in Florida are nonmigratory, but they experience an influx of migratory Burrowing Owls from the northern United States and Canada. Fall migration occurs in September and October, whereas spring dispersal is in March and May. Individuals can move as far as 180 miles overnight. One owl banded in Manitoba, was recaptured two months later in the Gulf of Mexico near Louisiana on an offshore oil rig. More research is needed to better describe the wintering areas of migratory Burrowing Owls to help conserve their northern and southern breeding (and nonbreeding) habitats because populations continue to decline in many areas due to habitat loss or alteration. In one study done in Saskatchewan, more than two-thirds of marked Burrowing Owls nested more than six miles from where they bred the year before.

The Burrowing Owl was commonly thought to be diurnal, but research found that they can forage anytime, day or night, especially when feeding large broods of rapidly growing young. Insects are most often captured during the day by either chasing after them on the ground, or by catching them in flight. Small mammals are hunted from perches at dawn or dusk, and they fly silently and erratically at their rodent prey, sometimes hovering overhead before pouncing. This owl is typically seen on raised areas or fence posts near the entrance to a burrow, watching for threats or prey. Their animated and exaggerated head movements help them judge distances, and when they feel threatened they flee quickly to hide underground in a burrow. Adults also watch the threat from the burrow entrance and will sometimes fly from one burrow to another to escape predators. They commonly roost in the entrance to a burrow or in other depressions in the ground, such as ditches. In Florida, they are sometimes seen roosting in trees.

Despite nesting underground, this species is vulnerable to some predators like the American badger, which is able to dig them out. Other threats to Burrowing Owls include collisions with motor vehicles and

predation by Short-eared and other owl species, as well as hawks, skunks, cats, dogs, snakes, and armadillos.

The Burrowing Owl eats invertebrates, including scorpions, beetles, earwigs, crickets, locusts, and grasshoppers, as well as small vertebrates such as amphibians, lizards, snakes, sparrows, larks, mice and young rats, bats, gophers, rabbits, and ground squirrels. In one summer, a family of Burrowing Owls can consume as many as 1,500 small rodents and 10,000 insects.

This owl is named for its strange behavior of nesting in abandoned burrows of ground squirrels or badgers in grassland habitats. Traditionally, they coexisted with (now extirpated) plains bison or

buffalo—hence their ready acceptance of cattle grazing on extensive prairie ranches on the Great Plains. Their curious habit of lining their nests, including the entrance, with dried cow or bison dung puzzles researchers, as it does not seem to influence nest success. Burrowing Owls in Florida dig their own nest tunnels. Up to twelve white eggs are laid in March or April and take about thirty days to hatch. Young owls stay in the burrow for fourteen days, and then near the burrow for over forty days before leaving the nest area. Family groups sometimes move to other burrows when young owls are mobile. Young can forage for insects when about fifty days old. The male cares for the young after they fledge, and some females are known to abandon them, continue migration farther north, then nest again with a second male in the same breeding season.

The Burrowing Owl occupies dry and open native grassland, savanna, and desert habitats, and also agricultural, ranch, and grassy road right-of-ways, residential areas, and airports where burrowing animals exist, especially prairie dogs, foxes, ground squirrels, and badgers. In the Andes it lives in open, arid sites up to 14,760 feet. Breeding home ranges average 600 acres and often overlap, with nest burrows sometimes only fifteen yards apart. Even so, male Burrowing Owls vigorously guard their nest entrances from other males and predators.

Its global status is least concern due to its large range and population. The loss of 99 percent of North America's prairie dog habitat, and the extinction of a large locust prey species during the 1900s, has greatly impacted this species. The grasshopper poison Carbofuran was banned in Canada in 1995 due to its impact on Burrowing Owl reproductive success. Its population has been declining over the last forty years. It is listed as threatened in Mexico, endangered in Canada, and has a special conservation concern status in parts of the United States. Conservation programs where landowners maintain grazing pastures for Burrowing Owls can safeguard local populations. In the Canadian prairies, over 700 grazing agreements have been negotiated by conservation organizations.

Boreal Owl
Aegolius funereus

The Boreal Owl is one of the most sexually reversed, size-dimorphic owls, which means that the females are significantly larger than the males. The top of this small owl's large umber-brown head is adorned with tiny white spots. Its yellow eyes, white eyebrows, and ivory to yellow-brown bill are set in a gray-white facial disk that has a blackish-brown border. It is named after the Greek god of the north wind, Boreas, and is also known as the Tengmalm's Owl in Europe, in honor of Swedish naturalist Peter Tengmalm. It was originally described in 1758, and its scientific species name is derived from the Latin word for "funeral." Other common names include the Pearl Owl and Richardson's Owl.

Total Length
7.9–11.8 inches

Wing Chord (unflattened)
6.1–7.6 inches

Tail 2.9–4.5 inches

Weight 3.2–6.8 ounces

The male's main song is a sequence of sixteen "hooh" or "poop" notes strung together in a trill, with a three- to four-second break between trills. He utters this call for many hours each evening, starting at dusk, within 650 feet of a nest tree cavity, in order to entice a female. Less commonly heard is the female's fainter, higher-pitched version of this call. Boreal Owls tend to stop calling when it is snowing or raining heavily, or during high winds. Males will also typically stop singing as soon as they attract a mate, or at least until she lays eggs. When a male approaches its mate in the nest cavity it utters a "wood" or "wood-whoohd" call, and the female may answer with a high-pitched "seeh" or "zuihd." Aggressive owls emit a whiplike "zjuck" or "jack" sound, or a hoarse "oohwack" and "kraihk" notes.

It lives in boreal forest habitats from eastern Canada to eastern Alaska and into Minnesota, to the south in montane-forested regions of the Rocky Mountains, and in other mountains south to New Mexico. It is also found in northern forests and in high-elevation forests in Eurasia. Northern populations partially migrate southward to the northern United States in winter in response to cyclic prey population declines. While some

individuals are known to nest within 500 yards of where they hatched, most travel long distances to subsequent nesting areas.

The Boreal Owl is nocturnal except in northern latitudes in summer, when it must hunt during the long subarctic days in order to catch enough food to raise its rapidly growing young. Boreal Owls typically hunt from low perches up to ten feet above the ground, and precisely locate concealed prey using their extremely asymmetrical ears. They avoid predators and hot summer temperatures by roosting from sixteen to twenty feet high in dense tree canopies. They roost close to tree trunks and usually switch roost sites each day.

The life of a small owl is fraught with danger. Incubating female Boreal Owls are sometimes ambushed and eaten by Pine Martens and avian predators such as Goshawks, and Long-eared Owls occasionally kill and eat both young and adult Boreal Owls. Competition for rare, suitable nest cavities can take its toll on males defending their territories; a smaller male Northern Saw-whet Owl was observed killing a male Boreal Owl in a desperate fight over a woodpecker nest hole. Despite these risks, some Boreal Owls can survive for at least eight years in the wild. Many owls starve in late winter or early spring following a cyclic multiannual prey population crash. Such hungry owls are often observed near backyard bird feeders to catch birds or to hunt small rodents and shrews feeding on spilled birdseed.

A variety of small animals are eaten, including insects such as beetles, frogs, birds, and mammals—especially rodents such as lemmings, shrews, mice, and voles. Larger mammals that are rarely eaten include chipmunks, tree and flying squirrels, weasels, and young snowshoe hares. The presence of bats in their diet implies that they are quite adept at locating nocturnal prey either in flight or at their secluded roosts.

Male Boreal Owls select breeding territories based primarily on the availability of one or more suitable nesting cavities. A female attracted to the area by the singing male selects the cavity and then lays up to ten white eggs in it from late March to early June. The female is fed by the male while she incubates the eggs alone for up to thirty days. Rarely, a male may entice a second female to nest within his territory provided that prey is abundant, but secondary nests are often not as successful as the primary nest. Young leave the nest cavity when they're about three to four weeks old, and are fed by the parents for an additional six weeks. Boreal Owls use a variety of older mixed-wood forested habitats throughout their range, including those with fir, tamarack, birch, poplar, spruce, and aspen trees in the boreal forest region and montane subalpine forests up to and over 9,800 feet. They hunt in open forests and along forest edges, including the areas adjacent to old weedy farm pastures and clear-cut forest stands. Prey availability, breeding status, and other factors influence an individual owl's home range size, which is known to vary from 500 to 6,000 acres in Colorado.

Its global status is least concern due to its large range and population. While it is the most common owl in many parts of North America, some isolated montane populations in Idaho, Wyoming, Colorado, New Mexico, Washington, and Oregon are of conservation concern. Protecting large live or dead trees with suitable nest cavities is recommended, as it can take up to 200 years for such trees to grow large enough for use by nest-building woodpeckers. Roosting habitats are also important to conserve as cleared forest areas in montane will be avoided by Boreal Owls for as long as 100 years.

Northern Saw-whet Owl
Aegolius acadicus

This diminutive owl has yellow eyes and a black bill set in a pale brown facial disk. The large, round head has no feathered ear tufts. It was first described in 1788 by Johann Gmelin. Its species name refers to the European colony of Acadia (now Nova Scotia) where settlers first saw it. Three subspecies are recognized, including the unique buff-colored and nonmigratory subspecies *Aegolius acadicus brooksi* found on the Queen Charlotte Islands of British Columbia. Other common names include the Acadian, Blind, White-fronted, and Farmland Owl.

Primarily nocturnal, it is most often detected by its song, which is similar to the warning beeps of a large truck backing up. Named for the sound of handsaw teeth being sharpened (or whetted) with a file, its main song is a rhythmic series of whistlelike "tewt" or "toot" notes. Members of a mated pair keep in touch by uttering either a two- to three-second whiny nasal call, or a three-note series of squeaky, terse, and loud contact call notes denoted as "ksew" or "skreigh-aw," which it also gives during migration. The call of the Queen Charlotte Islands subspecies is similar, but higher-pitched.

It breeds from Oaxaca, Mexico, north to the western and northeastern United States, and across southern Canada to southern coastal Alaska. Since the early 1900s, biologists have commented on the

Total Length
  6.7–9 inches
Wing Chord (unflattened)
  4.9–5.8 inches
Tail 2.6–2.9 inches
Weight 1.9–4.4 ounces

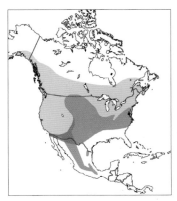

migratory habits of this tiny owl in the northern parts of its range. Its migration appears to be female- and juvenile-biased, with territorial males perhaps more reluctant to leave suitable nesting cavities. Some owls likely remain on their home ranges year-round, but large numbers congregate during the spring and fall migration on the shores of large water bodies, often along points of land jutting into lakes. Banded owls have been recaptured over 600 miles away during migration.

Its cryptic brown and white plumage and small size allows it to hide from most predators and humans by day. Often, the sound of songbirds scolding or mobbing an owl nearby gives away the owl's sometimes very low daytime roosts. It normally roosts in dense shrubs and tree foliage in sunlight, but also occasionally in buildings where its discovery surprises both the owl and the person finding it. Breeding males switch roost sites each day, whereas nonbreeding birds will often use the same roosts for many weeks, or even months. It is usually strictly nocturnal, and can locate, and subsequently capture, prey using sound alone with its extremely asymmetrical ears. It usually hunts from low perches.

Sometimes it appears at bird feeders in cold winter months during daylight hours, seemingly desperate for prey such as the small mammals feeding on spilled seeds, or the seed-eating birds attracted to the feeder.

The Northern Saw-whet Owl mainly eats small mammals such as mice and shrews, but also insects, spiders, and small birds. The Queen Charlotte Islands subspecies sometimes relies heavily on intertidal marine invertebrates called amphipods. It can kill prey up to four times its weight, such as Norway rats, flying squirrels, and pigeons.

169

It lays up to seven eggs, usually in tree cavities—often former woodpecker nest sites, from March through July. The male provides the female with food while she incubates up to twenty-nine days, and then while she broods the hatched chicks until they can generate their own body heat at about eighteen days old. Female Saw-whets can be quite protective of their nests. On occasion, I have had to nudge a female gently aside to count the eggs or young, all the while she was grasping my hand with all eight of her sharp black talons. When not disturbed, nesting females will sometimes dash out of the nest cavity to quickly bathe in nearby streams. Young leave the nest when they are about thirty days old, and the male continues to feed them for another thirty days. Polygyny, when a male will pair up and nest with more than one female in separate nest cavities, has been documented, but it is rare and occurs only in years when there is an ample prey supply.

Its typical habitats include middle-elevation riparian woodlands, coniferous and deciduous forests and woodlands, and sometimes in subalpine forests from sea level up to 11,550 feet. Mature or old-growth forests are either preferred, or are used frequently because they provide more cavity-nesting opportunities. Its territory size ranges up to 950 acres. The Northern Saw-whet Owl is perhaps the most common owl in North America, and its global status is least concern.

Unspotted Saw-whet Owl
Aegolius ridgwayi

Total Length
7.1–8.3 inches

Wing Chord (unflattened)
5.2–5.8 inches

Tail 2.5 inches

Weight 2.8–3.2 ounces

The Unspotted Saw-whet Owl has yellow eyes, a dusky bill, a white chin, and lores, and broad eyebrows set in a brownish facial disk with a dark rim. Anastasio Alfaro first described it in 1905. It was officially recognized as a full species in 1988. It is also called the Southern Saw-whet Owl. The territorial and courtship song of this owl is a series of four to ten "toot toot toot" notes that is often confused with the song of tree frogs. It also utters an assortment of high-pitched hissing "ssirrr" and "wreeei" shrieks.

The Unspotted Saw-whet Owl is endemic to southern Mexico through Guatemala to northeastern El Salvador, and central Costa Rica south to northern Panama. It is likely nocturnal and solitary during the nonbreeding season and has an agile, fluttering flight with fast wing beats. It is the smallest of the owls that share its forested environment, including the Northern Pygmy Owl and Mottled Owl, suggesting that it likely competes, and could fall prey to, other owls. There is no data on longevity, but similar-size owls are known to live for seven years in the wild. It likely eats a variety of invertebrates such as katydids, as well as small birds and mammals such as shrews, mice, voles, and perhaps bats.

There is little information on its breeding biology, but it likely uses tree cavities built by woodpeckers, or those resulting from decay and disease, for nesting. It reportedly lays between five to six white eggs. Breeding may commence in March; young—and a female with brood patches—have been noted in July. This owl uses the forest canopy, edges, and gaps to find its prey. It lives in damp pine-oak, oak, and cloud forests from 4,600 to 9,850 feet. The Unspotted Saw-whet Owl is thought to be territorial based on its rapid response to the imitation or playback of its song. Its global status is least concern. Forest habitats within its range are being damaged or destroyed and it is listed as being in peril of extinction in Mexico. Remaining habitats are limited to high elevations, steep slopes, or remote areas difficult to access.

Jamaican Owl

Pseudoscops grammicus

Total Length
  10.6–13.4 inches
Wing Chord (unflattened)
  7.8–9 inches
Tail 3.8–5.2 inches
Weight No data available

The Jamaican Owl is yellowish-brown with long, dark ear tufts. Its eyes are brown with whitish eyelids. Its light cinnamon face is edged with an inner thin white border adjacent to an outer dark rim. Its bill is yellowish-gray. It was first described by Philip Henry Gosse in 1847 based on a specimen collected in Tait-Shafton, Jamaica. More molecular genetic research is needed to determine its relationship to *Asio* owls. Based on differences in its skull, it is the only member of the genus *Pseudoscops*. When it gives its territorial call, a low gravely and muffled growl-like "to-whoo" sound, its normally tawny throat area expands and appears white. This is heard repeatedly with many seconds between calls. Another call is a "k-kwoarrr," or a rough-sounding, froglike croak. It has similar contact calls as the Long-eared and other *Asio* owls. This latter call is also uttered by hungry young demanding food, and is a high-pitched, drawn-out "kwe-eeh" squeak ending with an upturned inflection.

It is endemic to the island of Jamaica. Most or all of the 4,181 square miles of this island constitute its entire global distribution. It is nocturnal and roosts hidden by day in thick vegetation. Its habit of repeatedly using the same roosts may be a result of limited roosting opportunities due to habitat loss. The Jamaican Owl eats beetles and other large insects, spiders, tree frogs, lizards, smaller birds, and rodents.

Starting in December, up to three white eggs are laid in tree cavities. Forested or woodland habitats are used, including agricultural landscapes and smaller gardens with fragmented, treed areas. These must contain at least one or a few larger or older trees with suitable nest structures to support a breeding pair. Open savannah or older forests, and dense forests adjacent to grassy or weedy fields, provide edge habitats used for hunting. Lowland and mid-elevation habitats are thought to support denser populations than montane regions. Its global status is least concern. Ongoing deforestation, domestic cats, and hunting threaten its survival. The protection and restoration of Jamaica's forests is necessary to conserve this beautiful owl that is found nowhere else in the world.

Stygian Owl

Asio stygius

Total Length
15–18.1 inches

Wing Chord (unflattened)
11.5–15 inches

Tail 6.5–7.8 inches

Weight 1.3–1.5 pounds

This medium-size owl has yellow eyes, white eyebrows, and a black bill set in a blackish facial disk. Johann Wagler described it in 1832 based on a specimen from Brazil. It is also called the Devil's Owl due to its light-reflecting red eyes and its hornlike ear tufts. Its official common name, Stygian, is derived from the river Styx of Greek mythology, which separates the underground world of the dead from that of the living world. A low-frequency "whuof" is uttered by males and is repeated for long periods with as much as ten seconds between notes. Interested females will respond with a catlike "miah." Other rough or harsh notes are voiced by upset or excited owls.

The Stygian Owl is found discontinuously from northern Mexico to northern Argentina, including islands in the Caribbean such as Cuba and Hispaniola. It is mainly nocturnal, roosting among dense tree canopy foliage by day. Hunting usually occurs from perches, but they likely catch some insects, birds, and bats while flying. Very few longevity records exist, and most young likely perish in their first year of life. Adults then typically survive for only one or two years, but occasionally some individuals survive for one or (rarely) two decades. Prey eaten includes grasshoppers, dung beetles, and other insects; crustaceans; amphibians; reptiles; birds; and mammals, including bats. Males slowly clap their wings together a few times below the body to court females. Breeding occurs from March through September and the typical clutch size is two eggs, which are occasionally laid on the ground, but more commonly in trees in stick nests built by other birds.

It can be found in thorn scrub, pine plantations, and wooded habitats, including a mosaic of patchy openings as one would find in parks. In Texas, it has been found in forested floodplains of the Rio Grande. It ranges from sea level up to 10,170 feet. Its global status is least concern due to its large range. It is thought to be common in western Mexico and Belize, and rare farther south into Colombia and on islands in the Caribbean. Habitat destruction at lower elevations has restricted its population in montane pine, pine-oak, and cloud forests in some areas.

Long-eared Owl

Asio otus

This is a medium-size owl with golden-yellow eyes and a black bill set within a distinctive orange-buff facial disk. There are black patches adjacent to the inner sides of the eyes, and prominent white eyebrows. It has a large, round head and noticeable ear tufts when perched. In flight, however, the ear tufts are laid back against the head and are hard to see. Males are somewhat lighter than females. The grayish-white and light brown underparts have dark brown streaking and barring, while the upper parts are a mottled mix of white, gray, buff, brown, and black. The feathered legs and toes end with slender black talons. It was first described by Carolus Linnaeus in 1758. As many as four subspecies are currently recognized, but some taxonomic authorities consider the African Long-eared Owl (*Asio abyssinicus*) to be an additional subspecies of the Long-eared Owl. Local common names include the Cat Owl and the Coulee Owl.

The male Long-eared Owl's spring song is a series of more than ten, sometimes hundreds, of deep, monotonous "hoo" notes spaced about two to four seconds apart. Females can be heard uttering a nasal and soft "shoooogh" note every two to eight seconds near hooting males, or from the nest. Males also fly slowly by, and around, perched females while periodically bringing their wings together under their body, making a slow clapping sound. This latter display is also used in aggressive

Total Length
    13.8–15.8 inches
Wing Chord (unflattened)
    9.9–12.6 inches
Tail 4.7–6.3 inches
Weight 0.46–0.95 ounce

encounters. Both sexes give alarm calls, including a barking "ouurak ouurak ouurak" when predators approach their nest or fledged young, and a moaning catlike or foxlike "wawo" call. It is unnerving to sometimes hear this latter call when holding an owl while it is being banded.

The Long-eared Owl has a wide distribution in North America, from the northern boreal forest tree line in the Yukon and the Northwest Territories, and from Alaska to subtropical Mexico. An estimated 25 to 50 percent of its population resides in Eurasia, making it one of a few owl species with a circumpolar range. It can overwinter in snow-free parts of its range, but more northern populations, including those nesting in most of Canada and in the north-central United States, migrate from late September to late November to locate accessible prey supplies. One banded owl flew 2,500 miles from Saskatchewan to Oaxaca, Mexico. Local breeding populations can fluctuate dramatically with the availability of small mammal populations, especially meadow voles. The tracking of prey densities by this nomadic predator is facilitated by their habit of communal roosting outside of the breeding season. Short-eared and Long-eared Owls are occasionally found sharing winter roost sites. Some island and mainland populations of Long-eared Owls in warmer latitudes may be less migratory, or even year-round residents. For example, in one study in Idaho, four males nested 500 to 1,500 yards from where they originally hatched.

It is primarily nocturnal, roosting by day in dense foliage, except when the demands of feeding numerous, rapidly growing owlets can push a breeding adult to hunt well into the morning after dawn, or start hunting well before dusk, when summer days are long and evenings are short. The presence of breeding adults in June or July is often first discovered when they are intensively mobbed while hunting in daylight by robins and many other types of birds. This reaction from such birds is warranted as Long-eared Owls eat significant numbers of birds, with many taken at night from their roosts while sleeping. It can capture such prey in near-complete darkness by sound alone. Coordinated or cooperative hunting of two birds has been observed, where a lead owl flew fast along a hedge, flushing panicked birds hiding therein out of the hedge and into the waiting talons of the second bird, trailing closely behind its partner.

The longevity record for a wild Long-eared Owl is an astonishing twenty-seven years and nine months, longer than that recorded for captive owls. Many are killed by collisions with vehicles, and, to an unknown extent, barbed-wire fences take their toll on local populations. Raccoons frequently take eggs and nestlings. It also falls prey to Barred and Great Horned Owls.

Small birds and mammals, especially rodents such as voles and mice, comprise the diet of this species. One recent Long-eared Owl diet review study summarized over 800,000 prey items gleaned from data within 312 scientific publications. Over 470 species of prey were tallied, including 191 types of birds, 180 mammals, 83 invertebrates, 15 kinds of reptiles, 7 amphibian species, and 1 type of fish. Most prey were estimated to be less than 1.8 ounces, with the largest prey taken estimated to be 1.1 pounds. The diet of this opportunistic predator varies considerably in different locations.

From mid-March to mid-May anywhere from two to ten, but more commonly four to five, eggs are laid in stick nests built by crows, magpies, hawks, or herons in dwarf-mistletoe brooms, and sometimes atop leafy squirrel nests in large shrubs or dense trees. Atypical nest sites include a simple depression on the ground, in tree cavities, and rarely on cliff crevices. Some nests are used repeatedly for many years, and it will also nest in artificial nest platforms constructed and placed for owls in suitable habitats. It is typically monogamous. The eggs are incubated by the female for twenty-five to thirty days, and young leave the nest at twenty to twenty-seven days, before they can fly when they are about thirty-five to forty days old. They gain independence when two months old, and can breed the following spring. A mix of wooded stands and grassy and weedy habitats provide this owl with both nesting and foraging opportunities. It nests in forested locations adjacent to its preferred hunting habitats, including open wooded areas, old fields, riparian areas, shelterbelts, marshes, farmland, and scrubby deserts. It is found in habitats ranging from sea level to greater than 6,600 feet. Neighboring nesting pairs have been found as close as 46 feet. The densest breeding concentrations recorded is one pair per five square miles, but it is usually less. Home range size varies from 84 to 262 acres. Communal winter roosting is another trait that confirms the highly social nature of this owl, with as many as 100 individuals reported in tightly clustered trees.

The IUCN lists the Long-eared Owl as least concern, or not at risk, due to its extremely large global range and a population size estimated to be between one and a half to five million owls worldwide. Data from the North American Breeding Bird Survey and Christmas Bird Count has documented a small or statistically insignificant decrease over the last forty years in North America. It is difficult to detect statistically significant population size trends for species whose numbers are cyclic, or that undergo multiannual fluctuations in response to varying prey abundance, therefore actual population trends are not known. The continued loss of forested woodlots and treed riparian nesting areas to housing developments, and of hunting habitats such as marshes and grasslands to agriculture, is a threat to many populations. The Long-eared Owl has been assessed as critically imperiled in nine states, including Ohio and Kentucky, and as imperiled in three Canadian provinces as well as twelve states in the United States. Elsewhere in Canada and the United States, it is assessed as vulnerable to secure. Fatal poisoning of Long-eared Owls that ate rodents killed with the organophosphate Azodrin or Dieldrin has been cause for concern due to the continued use of such toxic compounds in some areas.

Striped Owl

Asio clamator

Total Length
11.8–15 inches

Wing Chord (unflattened)
9–11.6 inches

Tail 5–6.5 inches

Weight 0.7–1.2 pounds

This medium-size owl has cinnamon-brown eyes and a black bill set in a black-bordered, but predominantly white, sometimes brownish, facial disk. Its buff-edged black ear tufts are noticeably long compared to other Long-eared Owls. Louis Jean Pierre Vieillot was the first to publish a scientific description of this owl in 1807. Genetic research is needed to determine the evolutionary relationship between this and the similar Jamaican Owl.

The Striped Owl's song is a one-second-long, single nasal hoot— "hooOOOoh"—that is higher-pitched and louder in the middle. The female's higher-pitched voice is evident when mates utter a chorus of seven to eight barking notes depicted as "hu-how how how," which is sometimes low, and muffled "kiff" hoots.

It is reported to be a year-round resident that hunts at night, flying low over open habitats or from tree stumps, fence posts, or utility wires along roads. Up to twelve individuals have been seen roosting together in the nonbreeding season, but otherwise it roosts singly by day on the ground, or in low brush.

While rodents and other small mammals are its main prey, insects, snakes, and birds such as doves are also eaten. One study of twenty-eight pellets identified that exotic rats (five), and mice (thirteen), comprised 68 percent of the thirty-one identified prey items, but it also identified two native rodents, one frog, seven cockroaches, and three crickets in the sample.

From December to March it lays its two to four eggs in depressions on clumped grass or on the ground, at the base of palm leaves, or in low tree cavities. It lives in rain forests, riparian woods, savannahs, grasslands, and marshes, including developed areas such as suburbs and farmlands, ranging from marine coastal to montane, up to 5,250 feet above sea level. However, within these varied habitats, it has an affinity for open areas, and appears to colonize habitats opened up by logging activities.

Its global status is least concern due to a lack of substantial threats throughout its expansive range. The local use of rat poison may threaten local populations.

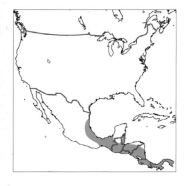

Short-eared Owl

Asio flammeus

Total Length
13–17 inches

Wing Chord (unflattened)
11.1–13.2 inches

Tail 5.1–6.2 inches

Weight 0.5–1.1 pounds

In areas of North America with no (or relatively little) snow cover, one can sometimes see congregations of Short-eared Owls silently flying over grassy fields, like a large butterfly ballet in the early dawn or at dusk. And it is at this time that its Latin name *flammeus* makes sense, for its reddish feathers seem to burst into flames when the sun is likewise fiery red at sunset and sunrise. Its black bill and bold yellow eyes, set in black orbits, are framed by a whitish-gray facial disk. The large, round head is topped by small, feathered ear tufts in the center. In 1763 Erich Pontoppidan, a Danish naturalist and bishop, wrote the first scientific description of this species. It is also called the Prairie, Marsh, and Bog Owl.

Males utter a raspy doglike barking alarm call: "wrawk, wrawk, wrawk," mixed with a loud "iii-yurp." Their main song is a long series of thirteen to eighteen short "hoo" notes, which is delivered during a dramatic undulating flight display from just above the ground to 1,150 feet. Females sometimes utter a "keeeyup" call in response. The male also makes a series of rapid clapping sounds by hitting the wings together under his body while in a steep downward dive toward a female on the ground below.

It breeds from the Arctic prairies to southern Canada, and in the northern United States from Northern California east to Virginia.

Populations found north of the U.S.-Canada border migrate south to winter in snow-free areas as far south as Mexico. A breeding population may be colonizing Florida, migrating across the ocean from the Greater Antilles. It nests in prairie or Arctic grasslands and marshes with good food supplies. Adults, but more so juveniles, can disperse almost 1,200 miles in under fifty days. Migratory owls often congregate near abundant rodent populations.

The Short-eared Owl hunts mainly at dusk and dawn, but also by day or through the night. They perch close together in winter communal tree roost sites, and such sites may also host roosting Long-eared Owls.

This opportunistic hunter seeks its prey while flying low, skimming the prairie grasslands, then turning quickly or hovering before falling onto a surprised vole, lemming, mole, pocket gopher, rabbit, shrew, or mouse. Birds taken include songbirds, gulls, terns, and shorebirds. It is known to prey on other owls, including the Burrowing Owl. Hills, mounds, fence posts, trees, and poles are sometimes used for hunting. Young owls develop their hunting skills by playing with inanimate objects such as rocks or clumps of earth, gradually progressing to catching insects and finally voles.

Female Short-eared Owls lay five to six eggs, but more (up to sixteen) in years when voles are extremely abundant, and at more northern latitudes. Nests consist of trampled grass on slightly elevated or well-drained ground. Breeding starts from March to early July. Breast feathers from the female's brood patch end up partially lining the scraped nest depression. Areas with grassy vegetation about twelve inches high are preferred, as such habitat provides at least some cover. Incubation lasts up to thirty-one days, and when the owlets are from fourteen to twenty-five days old they walk up to a quarter mile from their nest, usually in different directions. This dispersal occurs over a number of days. During this period the chicks remain hidden by prairie grasses and other plants. The adults care for their young until they are fifty days old, at which time they are old enough to hunt and migrate. Sometimes nests are less than 200 feet apart, and densities of one nest per 13.6 acres have been reported. Breeding habitats used by this owl include coastal, open, or slightly treed inland grasslands, and prairies, marshes, stubble fields, Arctic tundra, and subalpine meadows. In winter they use the same open habitats, but also gravel pits, clear-cut forests, and shrub thickets.

Its global status is least concern due to its large population and the largest worldwide distribution of any owl species. Its ground nests are vulnerable to skunks, foxes, cats, dogs, grassland fires, and hay harvesting. Habitat loss occurs when fertile grasslands are cultivated and marshes are drained. Owls that eat poisoned rodents either die or become sick. As a result, North American populations have declined significantly and it is listed as endangered, threatened or of special conservation concern in many parts of North America.

Index

Page numbers in *italics* refer to images.

Bibliography and Further Reading

Backhouse, F. *Owls of North America*. Firefly Books, Buffalo, NY, 2008.

Berger, C. *Owls*. Stackpole Books, Mechanicsburg, PA, 2005.

del Hoyo, J., A. Elliott, and J. Sargatal, Eds. *Handbook of the Birds of the World*, Volume 5. Barcelona: Lynx Edicions, Barcelona, Spain, 1999.

Duncan, J.R. *Owls of the World: Their Lives, Behavior and Survival*. Key Porter Books, Toronto, Canada, 2003.

Gehlbach, F.R. *The Eastern Screech Owl*. Texas A&M University Press, College Station, TX, 1995.

Hollands, D. *Birds of the Night*. Reed Books, Balgowlah, NSW, Australia, 1991.

Hollands, D. *Owls: Journeys Around the World*. Bloomings Books, Melbourne, Australia, 2004.

Hume, R. and T. Boyer. *Owls of the World*. Running Press, Philadelphia, PA, 1991.

Johnsgard, P.A. *North American Owls: Biology and Natural History* (Second Edition). Smithsonian Institution Press, Washington, DC, 2002.

König, C. and F. Weick. *Owls: A Guide to the Owls of the World* (Second Edition). Yale University Press, New Haven, CT, 2008.

Lawrence, R.D. *Owls: The Silent Fliers* (Revised Edition). Key Porter Books, Toronto, Canada, 2001.

Long, K. *Owls: A Wildlife Handbook*. Johnson Books, Boulder, CO, 1998.

Lynch, W. *Owls of the United States and Canada*. John Hopkins University Press, Baltimore, MD, 2007.

Marcot, B.G. *Owls of Old Forests of the World*. Gen. Tech. Rep. PNW-GTR-343. U.S. Dept. of Agriculture, Forest Service, Portland, OR, 1995.

Mikkola, H. *Owls of Europe*. Buteo Books. Vermillion, SD, 1983.

Mikkola, H. *Owls of the World: A Photographic Guide*. Christopher Helm, London, 2012.

Rashid, S. *Small Mountain Owls*. Schiffer Publishing Ltd., Atglen, PA, 2009.

Romulo, C.L. *Geodatabase of Global Owl Species and Owl Biodiversity Analysis*. M.N.R. Capstone Paper, Virginia Polytechnic Institute and State University, Church Falls, VA, 2012.

Sutton, P. and C. Sutton. *How to Spot an Owl*. Chapters Publishing Ltd., Shelburne, VT, 1994.

Tyler, H.A. and D. Phillips. *Owls by Day and Night*. Naturegraph Publishers, Inc., Happy Camp, CA, 1978.

Voous, K.H. *Owls of the Northern Hemisphere*. The MIT Press, Cambridge, MA, 1988.

Walker, L.W. *The Book of Owls*. Alfred A. Knopf, New York, NY, 1974.

birdlife.org
bna.birds.cornell.edu/bna/
globalowlproject.com
iucnredlist.org
neotropical.birds.cornell.edu
owlpages.com
planetofbirds.com

Acknowledgments

I dedicate this book to the indefatigable Deane P. Lewis, creator of The Owl Pages (www.owlpages.com), for his monumental efforts to make information on owls available to the world.

My first and greatest thank you goes to Patsy Duncan and our children, Connor and Brooke. I couldn't have completed this task without your full support and understanding. Patsy and I have been studying owls together since the day we first met in 1986, and it looks like there is more fun ahead! My in-laws, Jim and Nadia Lane, also deserve a big thank you for keeping our homestead in order and looking beautiful while I worked on this book.

In late 2012 I lured my almost 90-year-old former professor and fellow owl expert, Dr. Robert W. Nero, to my office one day by offering to buy him a cup of tea. After he finished drinking my bribe I passed him my draft manuscript and asked if he would read it over. To my delight he agreed, and I reassured him that he could take as long as he needed. Imagine my surprise when Bob returned to my office the very next day with his suggested edits handwritten over the entire manuscript! Thanks so much for that effort and for mentoring me over the decades, Bob.

I owe a big thank you to Frank Hopkinson, Publisher, and David Salmo, Senior Editor, Anova Books Group Ltd., for their assistance in scoping, guiding, and engaging me as an author in the creation of this book. It was a real pleasure working with you both.

Due to the book project timelines, I had to work on the manuscript during a two-week family vacation. For about two hours every day I found a suitable "office" location to plug in my laptop and spread out my reference materials and write. Thus, this book was written in coffee shops, restaurants, car repair garages, hotel rooms, and in the houses of friends and family in Manitoba, Ontario, Quebec, Minnesota, Wisconsin, and Michigan. Everywhere we stayed, without exception, people were helpful in accommodating my need to work on the book. Thanks to you all!

Like many authors I used a variety of printed scientific references, and those available on the internet, to write this book. What surprised me was the additional information and references I obtained by sharing my writing experience with friends and colleagues through online social media networks. This was in addition to the supportive and humorous comments from my social media friends that helped motivate me along the way. These included new friends such as Allison Gluck-Clarke and Stan Moore, and long-time associates such as Deane Lewis and John Triffo, to name but a few. Thanks for sharing your web search findings with me freely, and for your wit, insightful suggestions, and stimulating messages. You will all hopefully recognize your influence in this book.

The creation of this book was only possible due to the hard work and published technical research of many owl biologists and owl enthusiasts around the world. We owe these persons a debt of gratitude for their efforts building the foundation of knowledge on owls. Thus, we all get to see farther by standing on the shoulders of those who have gone before us. I hope that some of you will, after reading this book, be inspired to work toward the conservation of owls and owl habitat, to start to research and learn new things about these fascinating birds, and in the process help create a better world for owls!

Dr. James Duncan, Balmoral, Manitoba, Canada

Picture Credits

Alamy: 11, 14, 16, 24, 28, 29, 30, 35, 39, 40, 48, 50, 64, 65, 71, 99, 101, 104, 105, 128, 129, 141, 143, 147, 148, 152, 158, 159, 164, 168, 169, 173, 176, 183, 185.

Corbis: 9, 20, 33, 34, 41, 45, 47, 52, 54, 58, 59, 60, 61, 63, 67, 68, 75, 92, 94, 95, 98, 100, 107, 108, 116, 117, 118, 119, 121, 122, 125, 126, 130, 131, 133, 137, 150, 151, 153, 154, 155, 157, 162, 163, 167, 184, 186.

Getty Images: 2, 6, 7, 8, 10, 12, 13, 18, 19, 21, 22, 23, 25, 27, 31, 32, 36, 37, 42, 44, 46, 49, 53, 55, 56, 57, 62, 66, 74, 83, 91, 93, 96, 103, 106, 109, 113, 120, 123, 127, 132, 136, 156, 160, 161, 165, 166, 175, 177, 178, 179, 180, 181, 187.

Jenni Morgan: 15.
Dr. James R. Duncan: 38.
Chris Jimenez (www.chrisjimenez.net): 73, 81, 85.
Jorge Martin Silva Rivera: 77.
Dan Voydanoff: 79.
Pia Öberg: 86.
Julio Gallardo: 87.
Jose D. Alicea: 89.
Rolando Chavez Diaz Miron: 111.
Elí García & Haydée Morales: 115.
Richard C. Hoyer, WINGS Birding Tours: 135.
Dave Irving: 139.
Jeffrey Gordon: 145.
Knut Eisermann, CAYAYA BIRDING: 171.

All maps by David Watts.

WITHDRAWN